street food

from around the world

SUMACH PRESS

street food

Easy quick meals to cook at home   by Troth Wells

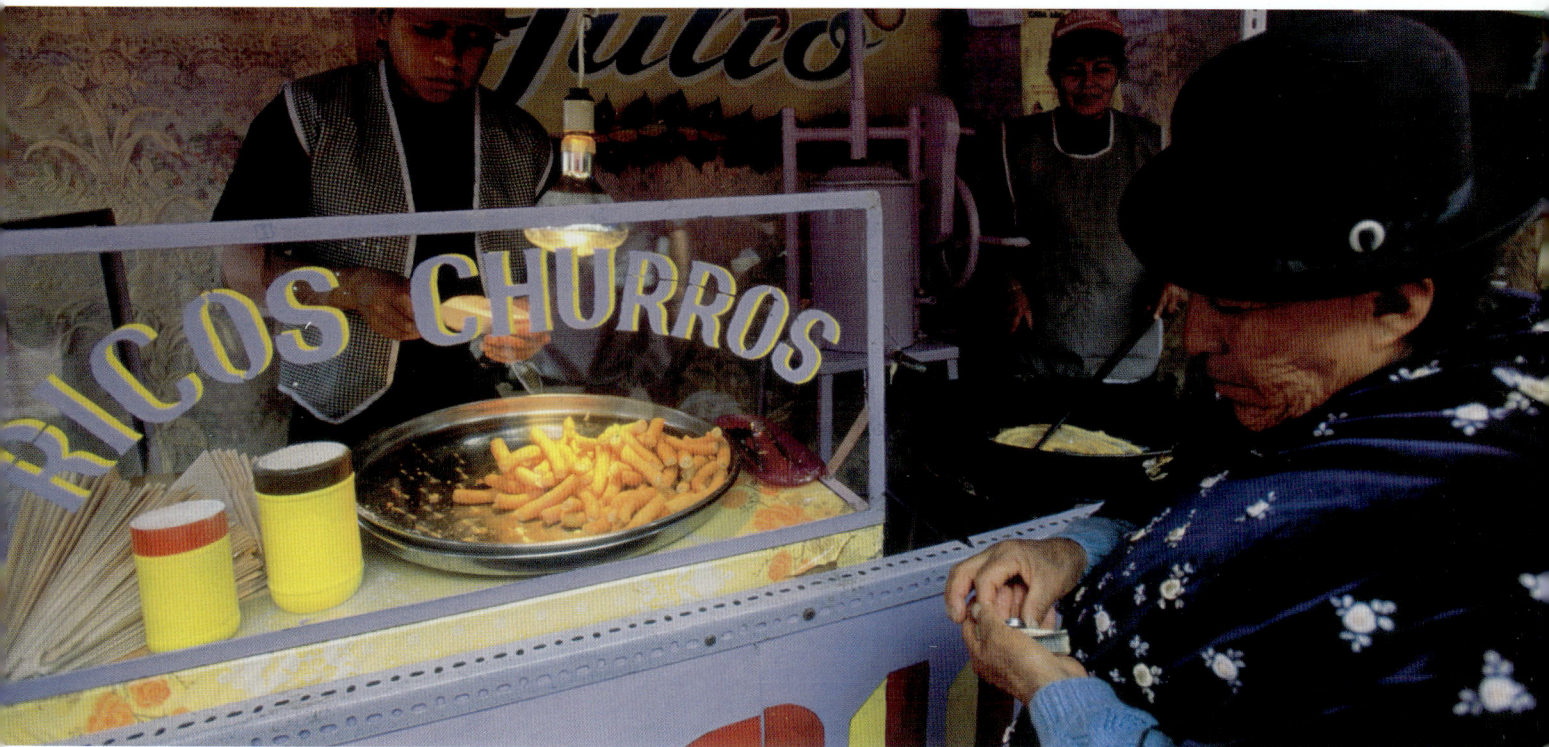

Churros stall, La Paz, Bolivia.

Library and Archives Canada Cataloguing in Publication

Wells, Troth
    Street food from around the world : easy quick meals to cook
at home / Troth Wells. -- Canadian ed.

First published 2005 under title: The world of street food.
Includes bibliographical references and index.
ISBN-13: 978-1-894549-57-8
ISBN-10: 1-894549-57-0

1. Quick and easy cookery. 2. Cookery, International. 3. Vegetarian
cookery. I. Wells, Troth. World of street food. II. Title.

TX833.5.W46 2006   641.5'55   C2006-902214-3

First published in the UK in 2005 by
New Internationalist™ Publications Ltd
55 Rectory Road
Oxford OX4 1BW, UK
www.newint.org

Food photography © Kam & Co., Denmark.
email: studiet@kam.dk
© all other photographs: individual photographers/agencies.

Text © Troth Wells/New Internationalist 2005 and individuals contributing.

Design by Andy Kokotka/New Internationalist.
Printed on recycled paper by south China, China.

Acknowledgements
First, special thanks to Dexter Tiranti, the inspiration behind the NI's books, for his drive,
creativity and support over many years.
    Thanks for their great enthusiasm, photos and information to Jacob Lotinga and
his English language students in China; also to José Elosegui, Hersilia Fonseca and
Patricia Pujol in Montevideo, Uruguay. Their excellent descriptions of food and places
helped transport me, in spirit at least, to the streets of Zhenjiang and parts of Latin
America.
    I'd also like to thank Anwar and Mahmuda Fazal, Susan Siew and friends in Penang,
Malaysia for their help. Thanks too, to Imran Mirza, Reem Haddad and all the people
who sent in recipes, explaining where and when they ate them; there are some fascinating stories. Ben Coren and Andy Kokotka both kindly remembered to find me recipes on
their travels. Dinyar Godrej provided several recipes, embellished with lovely descriptions of his childhood in India. In the long cold English August of 2004, William Beinart
kept me going with his enthusiasm and cooking skills as we tested the recipes. Thanks
also to Bev Laing, Andy Kokotka, Chris Brazier and other colleagues at the NI.

contents

Note: recipes marked 'V' are vegan; 'Va' are vegan-adaptable.
Most recipes are vegetarian or can be easily adapted.

Plates of fruit, Old Delhi, India.

Asli FO
DELICIOUSLY AFFOR
WOMEN'S SELF EMPLOYMEN
ACHANAK COLONY, MAHAKALI CAVES RD. ANDHERI(En
PHONE No. 00 91 22 28324692, TELEFAX
mail: create@bom5.vsnl.net.in, Website: ww

TOP LEFT Food stall in Penang, Malaysia.
TOP RIGHT Café in Havana, Cuba.
BOTTOM RIGHT Lunchtime at the World Social Forum, Mumbai, India.
BOTTOM LEFT Choice of street food, Zhenjiang, China.

the world of street food

'See that tree over there?' said Mohamed, pointing at a straggly specimen across the busy road in Penang's George Town. 'That was where my grandfather used to sell his *nasi kandar*. He had two baskets at either end of a pole that he carried on his shoulders to this spot. Then he'd unwrap one and set up his little fire. The second basket carried rice and other ingredients.

'In time, he did well enough to buy a hawker cart. My father took that on and the business grew, so that he was able to rent a stand in a coffee shop. And from that, here I am with nasi kandar stalls of my own.'

Mohamed's grandfather had come from Tamil Nadu, in India, along with many others. Many Tamils came as indentured laborers for the British, to work on Malaysia's rubber plantations. Others became hawkers, eking out a living in the towns, selling food and other goods.

Malaysia has a rich tradition in street food, not least because of its immigrant workers. The largest immigrant group in Malaysia is the Chinese, many of whom came to work on the country's tin mines. But an earlier wave of migrants – known as Nonya or Straits Chinese – had reached Malaysia in the early and middle part of the 19th century. Many married Malays, and fused their cooking ideas along with their genes to create some distinctive tastes and flavours.

'Malaysia is the street-food capital of the world,' said Anwar Fazal, when I explained the purpose of my visit. Anwar worked for years with consumer organizations – not testing fridges or driving the latest car, but setting up campaigning groups such as Pesticides Action Network, Health Action International and the International Babyfood Action Network, and working with the Consumers' Association of Penang, one of the foremost non-governmental groups.

These bodies turn the concept of a Western 'consumer' on its head, for they examine shopping and products in a different way, looking for example at what damage to workers and the environment is caused by agro-chemicals. They also focus on the well-documented scandal of baby-milk being sold to people who can neither afford it nor prepare it safely because they lack clean water. I'd worked with these organizations briefly in the 1980s and was pleased to be back again and see familiar faces. The excellent street food was of course another draw.

肉粽
大 RM1.80

肉粽
小 RM1.2[?]

MONTHLY MENU FOR NOODLES

1ST WEEK
MEE GORENG MAMAK
NASI GORENG

2ND WEEK
MEEUDANG

3RD WEEK
KUITEOW SOUP
BIHUN SOUP

4TH WEEK
LAKSA KAPITAN

Street food and stall, Penang, Malaysia.

McDonald's advertising, China.

Anwar had a treat in store: in my room was a copy of *Penang Food Odyssey*, a fascinating and detailed tour of the street food vendors and their specialities... you could almost hear the sizzle and smell the aromas.

The first thing to do is to visit each stall and see who is cooking what at this time of day. For some of the dishes are strictly breakfast fare, like *nasi lemak*, a Malay cuisine speciality. This is coconut rice and curry, with side dishes of fried anchovies, peanuts, hard-boiled eggs and cucumber. If you think that is an unusual combo to start the day with, then think how a plate full of fried egg, bacon, sausage and baked beans might seem to the uninitiated. *Nasi lemak* has a kick to get you going, supplied by chili.

From Accra to Bangkok and Mumbai to Mexico City, informal street trading is a way for many people to make a living. According to Britain's Natural Resources Institute 'street-vended food can contribute significantly to the food security of those involved in its production, particularly suppliers of raw produce, food processors and vendors.' The UN Food and Agriculture Organization (FAO) notes that 'selling snacks and meals on the streets is an important way to obtain income.' In Calcutta, selling street food is estimated to bring in almost $100 million per year for the 130,000 or so vendors, while in Latin America the monthly sales per vendor were around $150-500.

Most vendors are people who would otherwise be unemployed. Many women work in this sector – in some African countries over 80 per cent of those selling food on the street are women. This is a vital part of the economy, as women nearly always spend the cash on their families rather than on alcohol, sex or other diversions.

Making chapatis, Penang, Malaysia.

As well as making a living, the food hawkers and vendors provide cheap meals to thousands of people who may not be able to afford much else. Those queuing up for today's tasty dish may be schoolchildren, and some school canteens in Thailand and the Philippines buy in food from the hawkers.

Is there anything bad to say about this thriving and important industry? Well, there are health and hygiene concerns. Organizations such as the FAO are promoting clean water facilities and health checks for vendors. Malaysia, like some other countries, licenses vendors to ensure acceptable standards – and of course to keep an eye on who is doing what, where. In Zambia and Zimbabwe, hawkers are illegal but in times of economic hardship, people (both vendors and their customers) have few other survival options.

Local people and tourists alike can enjoy the colorful sights, delicious smells and bustle that surrounds the food hawkers – such as those busy at their stands in Penang's Gurney Drive, one of the city's most popular spots to eat.

Here, the way to find your favorite food is to go round the stalls and see for yourself what is being cooked. Most people speak enough English to understand what you are asking and will be pleased that you are showing interest in their cuisine. You order what you want and the various stallholders will bring the dish to you – go on, try several! The food is cheap and so good that quite often you will find Mercedes cars pulled up nearby, their occupants as keen on the wonderfully named *wanton mee* as the less well-wheeled foodies.

My favorite is *roti canai*, a Malaysian speciality. The stallholder who makes this is a star attraction as he whirls the dough, making it thinner and thinner, and slapping it down to cook on a hot griddle. It puffs up; you break off bits and dip them into the curry sauce. Totally delicious and highly addictive – an exquisite blend of the known and the exotic, just like Malaysia itself.

The recipes in this book have been adapted to make them easy to cook at home, and you can find most ingredients in the shops or specialty stores – or, now, on the web. And of course you can help support fair trade and organic producers by purchasing their goods – it really does make a difference.

Troth Wells

9

A F R

Fruit and vegetable stand, Egypt.

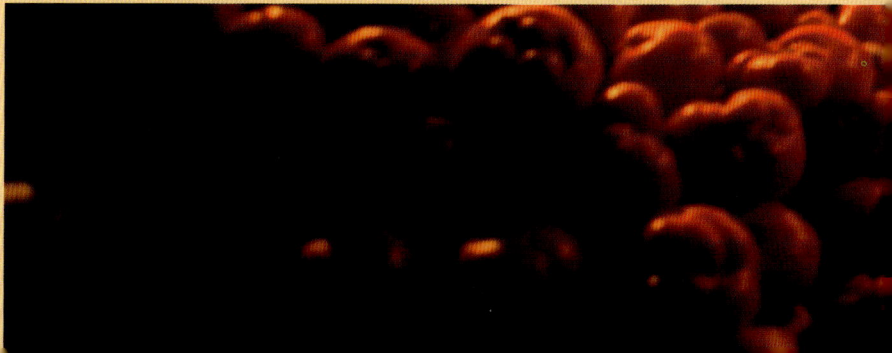

I C A

Lentil wat (stew) ^V

SERVES 4   PREPARATION: 10 MINUTES   COOKING: 20-30 MINUTES

Ethiopians may fast as many as 200 days a year, during which time they do not eat meat. This has led to many delicious vegetarian versions of the *wats* (stews). Light and lemony.

1 cup / 225 g lentils
1-2 onions, chopped
3 cloves garlic, chopped
1 teaspoon berbere* or 1 teaspoon chili powder
1 teaspoon fresh ginger, grated, or 1 teaspoon powdered ginger
3 cloves
½ teaspoon nutmeg, grated
juice of ½ lemon
1 tablespoon parsley or cilantro/ coriander, chopped
salt and pepper
oil

* Ethiopian spicy sauce, available in specialty stores.

Trader carrying butter in a gourd, Ethiopia.

1 Put the lentils in a pan with enough water to cover, and bring to the boil. Skim off any froth with a spoon, and then reduce the heat and simmer, covered, for 15-20 minutes until they are cooked and crumbly. They should have absorbed most of the moisture; if not, drain off the excess.

2 Now heat the oil in another pan and sauté the onions, adding the garlic after a few minutes when the onions are translucent.

3 Next, add the berbere or chili powder, the ginger, cloves, nutmeg and lemon juice. Stir well to combine the ingredients. Pour in a little water or oil if the mixture begins to catch.

4 Spoon the lentils into the spice mix and season. Cook over a gentle heat for 5-10 minutes to let the flavors expand, stirring frequently so that the mixture does not burn. Again, add more liquid if necessary to keep it moist. Garnish with parsley or cilantro/ coriander and serve with breads or rice.

Dabo kolo (fried snacks) Va

MAKES 20-24   PREPARATION: 20 MINUTES
COOKING: 10 MINUTES

Dabo means bread, and *kolo* is the word for roasted barley, which is eaten as a snack, like popcorn. *Dabo kolo* are popular in Ethiopia, eaten between meals, with drinks, and are available from street vendors and small shops. The snacks keep well and so are useful for people on the move. They are usually made from wheat flour, but can also be made from *tef* flour (used to make Ethiopia's famous flatbread, *injera*) or even chickpea flour.

1 cup / 100 g flour
¼ teaspoon salt
½ tablespoon sugar
¼-½ teaspoon berbere paste *
  or cayenne pepper
2 tablespoons oil
water
a little melted butter or margarine +

* Ethiopian spice paste
+ optional

1 Mix all the ingredients together, gradually adding a little water to form a stiff dough. Then knead for 5 minutes or so.

2 Next, take up pieces of the dough roughly the size of a walnut and press each one out on a lightly floured surface, using the palm of your hand, to make a long strip about ½ inch/1 cm thick.

3 Cut the strip into ½ inch/0.5 cm pieces. Repeat with the other dough strips.

4 Put the cakes on a pre-heated skillet/griddle or into a frying pan, with no oil, leaving a little space between them.

5 Cook over heat, turning occasionally, until golden brown. Leave to cool slightly and then serve plain, or with melted margarine or butter poured over if liked.

Mafé (peanut stew)

SERVES 6   PREPARATION: 30 MINUTES   COOKING: 20 MINUTES

Mafé, a traditional dish of the Wolof people of Senegal and Gambia, is one of the many variations of the African groundnut stew. The basic recipe uses meat, onion, palm nut oil, tomato paste, peanuts or peanut butter, some vegetables, chilies, bell pepper, salt, pepper and water. It is often made with lamb or mutton but can also use chicken, fish (fresh or dried) or substitute beans (such as black-eyed beans) for a vegetarian version. Chop and boil the vegetables first – then keep the stock to use in the dish.

1 pound / 450 g chicken, in pieces or ½ pound / 225 g cooked beans

2 onions, finely chopped

1 cup / 225 g peanut butter

1 red or green bell pepper, chopped

6 tomatoes, chopped

2 tablespoons tomato paste

1-2 chilies, left whole

2 cups / 300 g chopped vegetables, cooked, retaining stock *

water or stock *

½ cup palm oil/oil

salt and pepper

* Such as cabbage, carrot, potato, sweet potato, egg-plant/aubergine, squash or turnip.

1 Begin by heating the palm oil in a large cooking pot. Then sauté the chicken and remove the pieces when they are golden on all sides.

2 Now fry the onions in the same pan over a high heat. Next, put in the pepper, tomatoes, tomato paste and chilies. Fry for a few minutes before adding the water/stock, peanut butter and tomato paste. Stir to mix the ingredients and then simmer gently for a few minutes.

3 After this, add the chicken and the cooked vegetables. Season, and then leave to simmer, covered, for 30-60 minutes or until everything is cooked. Stir frequently and add more liquid if it becomes too dry. Serve with rice and sliced avocado or parsley.

Plasas or palaver stew

SERVES 4   PREPARATION: 15 MINUTES   COOKING: 40 MINUTES

1 pound / 450 g minced lamb
    or beef

2 onions, chopped

2 pounds / 1 kg greens,
    chopped finely *

1 red or green chili, de-seeded
    and chopped

1 red or green bell pepper,
    chopped

½ cup egusi or peanut butter

red palm oil or cooking oil

1-2 bouillon/stock cubes

water

salt and pepper

* For example, spinach, collards,
chard or kale.

Plasas or *palaver* stew, popular in West Africa, combines greens, meat and sometimes also dried fish with *egusi* (pumpkin seed paste), groundnut paste or peanut butter. *Plasas* is most often found in Gambia and Sierra Leone. Stock cubes and/or the ubiquitous Maggi sauce are widely used.

1 Start by heating the oil in a large pan and then brown the onions in it, adding the meat when the onions are transparent.

2 Next, put in the chili, bell pepper and stock cube with enough water to cover the meat. Bring to the boil and then turn down the heat to a simmer. Cook the meat for 20-30 minutes, or until tender.

3 Add the greens, cover, and cook until they are soft.

4 Mix the egusi or peanut butter into the ingredients and stir to combine. Simmer for a further 10 minutes and serve with rice.

Kalawule (spicy fried bananas) ^V

MAKES 16   PREPARATION: 5 MINUTES   COOKING: 5 MINUTES

Plantains or bananas are often fried without batter. *Kalawule – DoDo* in Nigeria – is one example, originally from Ghana and often sold by street vendors from trays in the evenings. A similar snack, but using sugar rather than spice, is *Zitumbuwa* from Malawi. If using dessert bananas you can shallow-fry them (see #3 below).

4 firm bananas, cut into chunks
½-1 teaspoon grated fresh or
**   powdered ginger**
½ teaspoon cayenne or chili powder
½ teaspoon ground black pepper
water
palm or peanut oil
salt

1 In a bowl, mix the ginger with the cayenne or chili, pepper, salt and a few drops of water to combine the ingredients. Stir.

2 Now put in the chunks of banana and coat them well.

3 Heat the oil in a deep-fryer or wok and cook the banana pieces in hot oil until nicely golden. Drain well on kitchen paper.

Cassava chips ^V

SERVES 2   PREPARATION: 5 MINUTES   COOKING: 10 MINUTES

I enjoy the roast maize available on the streets of Nairobi and most Kenyan towns. It is just white maize roasted over coals in the upturned lid of a garbage can – which is logical given that the hot coals are in the can underneath! The maize/corn can be eaten with any combination of salt, dry red pepper (chili powder) and fresh lemon juice squeezed over it – scrumptious. Available as a whole cob wrapped in old newspaper or telephone book pages and munched as you walk to or from work or stroll along the street.

The same vendor usually roasts cassava too, and runs a knife down the length of the piece of cassava to sprinkle in salt, dry red pepper and lemon before serving. From the coastal and lakeside towns of eastern Kenya comes the delicious dish of cassava crisps or chips, freshly deep-fried and sprinkled with – what else? – salt, dry red pepper and lemon juice. **Rajen Kantaria**

**½ pound / 225 g
  cassava root ***
chili powder
lemon juice
water
oil
salt

* Peel the cassava under cold running water as it discolors quickly.

1 Cut the cassava into ½-inch/1-cm slices. Put them in a saucepan with just enough salted water to cover. Bring to the boil and cook until they are tender, about 30 minutes. It does not matter if the pieces break up.

2 When they are cooked, remove from the water and drain; dry with paper towels.

3 Heat some oil in a frying pan or skillet and when it is hot, fry the pieces until they are crisp and golden all over. Sprinkle chili powder, salt and lemon juice over them. Serve at room temperature with drinks.

Maandazi V

MAKES 24   PREPARATION: 5 MINUTES   COOKING: 10 MINUTES

I lived in Kenya from 1987 to 1990. Originally a Swahili snack, *maandazi* – East African fried breads similar to donuts – are ubiquitous in *hotelis* (tea shops) all over the country. Like most things, they are best when fresh from the pan and make a delicious accompaniment to *chai masala* (spiced tea) for breakfast but can also be used to mop up a stew. **Frankie Meehan, Singapore**

¾ cup / 180 ml warm water
1 teaspoon baking powder
2 cups / 200 g plain flour
¼ cup / 60 g sugar
¼ teaspoon ground cardamom *
1 tablespoon margarine, melted
1 tablespoon warm milk
1 tablespoon beaten egg +
pinch of salt
oil for deep frying

* Or use cinnamon, allspice or ginger.
+ optional

1 In a large bowl, combine the flour, baking powder, sugar and spice.

2 Mix the water, milk and egg together with the melted margarine. If you prefer not to use the milk and egg, substitute water.

3 Gradually add this mixture to the flour, kneading into a smooth, elastic dough. Adjust with more flour/water as necessary to obtain the right consistency. Place the dough in a clean bowl and leave aside for about 15-30 minutes.

4 When ready, roll the dough to about ½ inch/1 cm thick. Then cut into triangles or small squares.

5 Heat the oil in a deep pan or wok. Slide each dough shape in (only fry as many as can float without touching each other). Once the bottom side is golden brown, turn them over and continue frying.

6 Remove the shapes with a slotted spatula and drain well on old newspapers or kitchen paper. Serve warm or cold, but do not store for more than half a day as they tend to go stale rather quickly. Sprinkle with icing sugar and cinnamon before serving.

Bunny chow V

SERVES 2   PREPARATION: 10 MINUTES   COOKING: 20 MINUTES

Despite its name *Bunny chow* has nothing to do with rabbits. It is the result of an only-in-South-Africa combination of Asian curry, European bread, and South African apartheid. 'Malay' slaves from Indonesia and Malaysia were brought to South Africa by the Europeans, and later were joined by indentured workers from India. The cuisine of these peoples mixed and by the early 20th century there were curry shops everywhere serving a bowl of curry with bread. As apartheid enforced segregation, restaurants did not serve black – African, Malay ('colored') or Indian – people. However they could sell take-away food, so an enterprising cook in Durban saw a way to keep custom by selling curry tucked into a half-loaf of bread (this was before paper or plastic plates). But why 'bunny chow'? Indian playwright Ronnie Govender suggests that eating houses in Grey and Victoria Streets in Durban served a distinctive Gujarati vegetarian dish called a *bhunia* and this gave rise to 'bunny'. And chow has meant 'food' since the Chinese workers built the mid-West railways in the US. Today bunny chow is so chic there are restaurants serving nothing else, using different breads flavored with pepper, garlic, cumin, aniseed and sesame. 'One of the few good things to emerge from apartheid,' say locals. **Congo Cookbook**

One of my favorites when I was a kid growing up in Durban, served out of the Himalaya Hotel. **David Johnson, Oxford, England**

Eating bunny chow, Durban, South Africa.

1 unsliced loaf of bread per two people
lentil curry *

* See p 68

1 Cut the bread into two halves. Using a plate or bowl, stand each half on its end and scoop out the middle.

2 Fill each half with curry. Use the scooped-out bread to mop up the curry and then eat the remainder with your fingers or a spoon.

Lesotho woman.

Ginger beer V

SERVES 2-4   PREPARATION: 5 MINUTES   COOKING: 10 MINUTES

This popular drink is by no means unique to Malawi or Africa – it is a favorite in some form or other in all the tropical regions. And some may remember a different drink: fizzy ginger beer in 'hot' British summers, in its familiar brown stone jars with the wired stopper tops.

½ cup grated fresh ginger
½-1 cup / 110-225 g molasses or sugar
3 cups / 700 ml water
4 cloves
juice of ½ lemon

1 First, boil the water. Then put the ginger into a bowl and pour on the boiling water. Cover and leave for at least one hour – overnight if possible.

2 When ready, strain the liquid off through a sieve or use a muslin bag. Press the ginger pulp to extract the flavor.

3 Add the molasses or sugar, the cloves and the lemon juice. Stir well to mix the ingredients. Taste, and adjust the flavors as desired, adding more water if required.

4 Leave the ginger beer to cool before serving.

Tchedoudiene (rice and fish)

SERVES 6   PREPARATION: 30 MINUTES   COOKING: 45 MINUTES

This is one of Senegal's classic dishes. There are almost as many different versions as there are names: *Ceebu Jën* (from the Wolof *ceeb*, rice; and *jën*, fish; pronounced cheb-o-djin) is also spelled *Ceebu Jen, Ceeb bu jen, Ceeb u jen, Thebouidienne, Thieboudienne, Theibou Dienn, Thiebou Dienn, Thiebou Dienne, Thiébou dieune, Tié bou dienne, Thieb-ou-Djien, Thiebu Djen* and sometimes just called *Thieb* or in French, *Riz au Poisson*. Feel free to add or remove some of the vegetables and experiment with flavorings.

6 steaks sea bass or other white fish fillets
2 onions, chopped
1 red chili pepper, de-seeded
3 cloves garlic, crushed
1 red bell pepper, chopped
4 tablespoons tomato purée
5 cups / 1.2 liters water
2 carrots, chopped
1 sweet potato, chopped
1 egg-plant/aubergine, chopped
1 cup / 100 g pumpkin or zucchini/
    courgette, cut in chunks
4 tomatoes, chopped
1 cup / 100 g cabbage, finely sliced
1 pound / 450 g rice
2 limes, cut in quarters
1 bay leaf
2 tablespoons cilantro/coriander or
    parsley, chopped
peanut or red palm oil *
salt and pepper

* If at all possible, use red palm oil – this gives a lovely color and flavor. It is available in Caribbean and specialty stores.

1 Chop half of one onion and half the red chili. Add garlic, 1 tablespoon of the cilantro/coriander or parsley and a pinch of salt. Pound the ingredients together in a mortar or use a blender until they form a paste. Make a small slit in each fish or fish fillet and stuff the paste inside.

2 Heat the oil in a large stew pot over medium heat. Chop the remaining onions and fry them in the oil. Add the stuffed fish steaks and fry until golden. Remove the fried fish steaks from the oil and set aside.

3 Stir the tomato purée and the water into the hot oil and bring the mixture to a boil. Mix in the carrots, sweet potatoes, and pumpkin if using and cook for 15-20 minutes. Add the remaining vegetables and the other half of the chili, salt, pepper and bayleaf. Simmer, covered, for 20 minutes. Put in the cooked fish for the last 5 minutes.

4 Turn off the heat. Ladle off most of the stew liquid into a pot and add the rice to this; bring to the boil and then simmer, covered, until the rice is cooked (add water if necessary). Keep the vegetables and the fish warm.

5 Spread the rice evenly across the bottom of a serving dish and heap the fish and vegetables in the center of the rice. Garnish with remaining parsley and serve with limes.

Koeksisters

MAKES 16   PREPARATION: 20 MINUTES   COOKING: 20 MINUTES

'Cooked sisters' – the 'sisters' may relate to the fact these donut-type snacks are usually plaited, suggesting close family ties, or girls with braids. *Koeksisters* originated in the Cape, introduced by the 'Malays' who were brought in as slaves from the 17th century, mainly from Indonesia. The Cape Malay cuisine blends dried fruit and spices to create wonderful flavors. By the way, this is your fat and sugar allowance for the week!

Children, Eastern Cape, South Africa.

1 cup / 100 g flour
½ teaspoon baking powder
1 teaspoon mixed spice
½ teaspoon ginger
¼ teaspoon salt
2 oz / 50 g butter or margarine
1 tablespoon beaten egg
oil

FOR THE COATING:
½ cup / 110 g sugar
½ cup / 120 ml water
cinnamon
juice of ½ lemon

1 Sift the flour, baking powder and salt into a bowl. Cut the margarine or butter into the mixture or rub until it is like breadcrumbs.

2 Now stir in the beaten egg; mix well and then knead the dough a little. When that is done, place the mixture on a floured surface and roll it out to ½ inch/1 cm thick.

3 Cut the dough into circles, triangles or make small balls. Set aside.

4 For the syrup coating, boil the sugar and water until thick, stirring all the time. Add some drops of lemon juice and ½ teaspoon cinnamon.

5 Heat the oil in a wok or deep-fryer and when it is hot, slide the koeksisters in carefully. Cook until golden; remove and drain on kitchen paper.

6 Place them on a plate, coat with the syrup and leave to cool.

Ful (beans)

SERVES 4   PREPARATION: 10 MINUTES PLUS OVERNIGHT SOAKING TIME IF USING DRIED BEANS
COOKING: 20-30 MINUTES (PRESSURE COOKER FOR BEANS)

This dish is also popular in Middle Eastern and other North African countries. In Sudan, it is the traditional all-day breakfast dish, available in tiny cafés, from street vendors and, most welcome of all, at bus stops in the desert. The ful beans are large flat brown beans (*fava* or field beans), resembling shiny dark brown butter beans, and *ful* is by no means fast food. At least 24 hours' soaking followed by 6 hours or so of slow cooking would be considered prudent. In Sudan, the beans are left to simmer overnight in fat-bellied, narrow-necked vessels on charcoal braziers, but canned beans can be bought in Greek or Turkish delicatessens.

The Sudanese traders bash the warm beans for a few moments with the base of an old glass fizzy drinks bottle to slightly break up the beans. A plateful is served with a variety of optional extras. A swirl of peanut oil, a handful of chopped fresh cilantro/coriander, salt and chili powder to taste is pretty standard. But the addition of a little grated feta cheese, chopped scallion/spring onion and a hardboiled egg would set you up for the day. The *ful* is usually eaten with flat bread, friends eating from a communal dish. **Pippa Pearce, London, England**

1 cup / 200 g fava or ful beans, cooked and
    kept warm
2 tablespoons fresh cilantro/coriander
2 hard-boiled eggs, sliced
2 scallions/spring onions, sliced
1 cup / 100 g feta cheese, crumbled
juice of 1 lemon
peanut or olive oil
salt

1 Place the cooked beans in a serving dish and crush them with the end of a rolling pin or spoon.

2 Pour over some oil and sprinkle on salt to taste. Garnish with the fresh cilantro/coriander.

3 Serve the eggs, scallions/spring onions and feta cheese separately, and hand round the lemon juice.

Mango fritters

MAKES 8   PREPARATION: 5 MINUTES   COOKING: 5 MINUTES

Tasty snacks of pieces of fruit, vegetable, meat – fritters turn up on just about every street food menu in the world – from *tempura* in Japan, to *pakoras* in India and apple fritters in Britain. They are popular snack food in Africa where they are often made with bananas, maize, pineapple or vegetable chunks. Mango is a tangy surprise.

2 mangos, peeled and cut into chunks
¾ cup / 75 g flour
1 egg, beaten
2-3 tablespoons milk
2 teaspoons sugar
oil

1 Begin by making the batter. Sift the flour into a bowl and add the sugar.

2 Take the bowl with the beaten egg in it and gradually pour in the milk, stirring as you do so. Then add this to the flour and sugar mixture.

3 Coat the mango pieces in the batter. Heat the oil in a deep-fryer or wok and when hot cook the mango pieces until they are just brown. Drain on kitchen paper.

A

Coffee shop, Penang, Malaysia.

SIA

中

室 餐 隆 敦

OP

KEDAI KOPI DAN MAKANAN

炒沙河米粉・雲吞麺
CHAR SAR HOR BEE HOON・WAN THAN MEE

粿條湯 KOAY TEOW THNG

Baozi (steamed filled buns) ^{Va}

MAKES 20-24 BUNS   PREPARATION: ABOUT 1 HOUR, PLUS 20 MINUTES RISING AND STANDING TIME
COOKING: 15-20 MINUTES

FOR THE DOUGH:
4 cups / 400 g self-rising flour
2 teaspoons dried yeast
1 tablespoon sugar
1 cup / 240 ml warm water

FOR THE SAVORY FILLING:
½ pound / 225 g mushrooms, finely chopped
½ pound / 225 g cooked pork or chicken +
**¾ cup / 125 g bamboo shoots, drained
    and chopped ***
2 scallions/spring onions, finely chopped
**1 teaspoon fresh ginger, finely chopped or
    use 1 teaspoon powdered ginger**
1 tablespoon rice wine
a little sesame oil
soy sauce
sugar
salt

+ optional – replace with cooked beans or chopped
vegetables such as carrots, or just use ready-made red
bean paste.
* Or use other vegetables such as bean sprouts.

I was working in Zhenjiang, Jiangsu province, along the Yangtze River (which makes it sound far more glamorous than it is). It's a medium-sized city – by Chinese standards, that means over 2 million people. The street food here is great – if you find the right part of town, among the older backstreets, there is a wealth of interesting food stalls. Across from the university is an area with little shops and simple restaurants that is also busy with food hawkers who assail you with their cries.

These popular buns are on sale from early morning. I quickly focused on the *doushabao*, as a sweet but fairly nutritious breakfast or snack food. They are filled with red bean paste – excellent for me as a vegetarian. At the *baozi* stall you can find other types of these buns, such as *roubao*, with meat, and *shucaibao*, filled with vegetables. **Jacob Lotinga, Beeston, England**

Baozi buns, China.

1 Begin by making the savory filling. Place all the ingredients in a bowl and mix well, adjusting the flavoring and seasoning to taste.

2 To make the dough, first dissolve the sugar and yeast in the warm water for 5-10 minutes until frothy.

3 Then sift the flour into a bowl, and gradually stir in the yeast mixture to make a firm dough. Knead for 5 minutes, cover with a damp cloth and leave in a warm place to rise for about 20 minutes.

4 When ready, remove the dough and knead it on a lightly floured surface for about 5 minutes before rolling it into a long sausage shape. Cut into 20 or so pieces and flatten each one with the palm of your hand. With a rolling pin, roll out each into a 4-inch/ 10-cm circle.

5 Place 1 tablespoon of the filling (either the red bean paste or the savory one) in the center of each flattened circle of dough. Now gather together the edges to meet at the top around the filling. Twist or press to enclose the filling.

6 Place the buns, seam side down, on a piece of aluminum foil or wax paper. Cover and leave to rise in a warm place for about 15 minutes.

7 When ready to cook, put the buns on foil on a steamer rack over boiling water. Leave at least 1 inch/ 2.5 cm between the buns. Cover and steam for 15-18 minutes, until done. Sprinkle with toasted sesame seeds if desired.

Bei gu su
(tofu/bean curd with vegetables) V

SERVES 4   PREPARATION: 15 MINUTES   COOKING: 10 MINUTES

A classic vegetarian stir-fry; easy and quick to make, tasty and nutritious to eat. By the way, 'julienne' sticks means cut really finely, like matchsticks.

1 pound / 450 g firm tofu, cubed
½ pound / 225 g snowpeas/mangetout
1 carrot, cut into julienne sticks
½ pound / 225 g mushrooms,
  finely sliced
4 scallions/spring onions, chopped
1-inch/2.5-cm piece of ginger, grated
1 tablespoon oyster sauce *
1 tablespoon rice wine or sherry +
2 tablespoons stock or water
1 teaspoon cornstarch
sugar
oil
salt and pepper

* Or soy sauce
+ optional

1 Heat some oil in a wok and fry the tofu until it is golden.

2 Carefully pour off any excess oil and then add the snowpeas/mangetout, carrot, mushrooms, 3 scallions/spring onions and the ginger. Stir-fry briskly for a couple of minutes, and then sprinkle on the oyster sauce and rice wine. Add sugar and salt to taste.

3 Pour on the stock or water and continue to cook. Mix the cornstarch with a little cold water to make a paste and then pour this into the pan, stirring to distribute it. Garnish with the remaining scallion/spring onion. Serve with rice or noodles.

Roti parcels

SERVES 4-6   PREPARATION: 10 MINUTES   COOKING: 30 MINUTES

'Roti parcels' – chapati or roti wrapped around a spicy filling (usually chicken, vegetable, or tinned fish) – are one of the most accessible quick lunches from street stalls in Fiji.

Gourmet fare it is not. Even so, it is a famous and authentic taste of urban Fiji, where imported tinned fish (especially mackerel) is not a substitute for reef-fish, but is seen as a culinary item in its own right, with its own distinct flavor. **Tim Adams, Rani Dhanjal, Noumea, New Caledonia/Kanaky**

6 rotis or chapatis, warmed

FOR THE FILLINGS:
2 tins tuna or 1 tin mackerel
2 cloves garlic, chopped
**1-inch/2.5-cm piece of
    ginger, grated**
1 onion, grated
½ teaspoon turmeric
½ teaspoon cumin

1 teaspoon mustard seeds
1 tablespoon tomato paste
1-2 chilies, left whole
1 teaspoon garam masala
¾ cup / 100 g peas
**1 tablespoon cilantro/
    coriander, chopped**
oil

1 In a frying pan over a good flame, add the oil. In this, fry the garlic and ginger together with the cumin and mustard seeds until the mustard starts to pop.

2 Now add the onion and fry a little longer until the onion is soft. Add some water or more oil if necessary to stop the mixture sticking. Next, put in the turmeric and tomato paste and combine well to form a paste.

3 After this, put in the fish, chili, peas and garam masala and cook until heated through. Season.

4 Remove the chili and then put spoonfuls of the mix in the center of the warmed roti/chapati. Scatter some cilantro/coriander leaves on top before wrapping the parcel up.

Spiced chai (tea) V

MAKES 2 CUPS   COOKING: 5 MINUTES

During my contract in India, I took detailed notes on how to prepare a good *chai*. Every stall there has its own recipe, which depends entirely on the spices used. It is fairly replicable outside of India, except for the actual tea. They use what I came to know as 'tea dust', which looks like little balls of tea and has a very distinct and much stronger flavor. The tea's flavor completely depends on the combination of cardamom, cloves, cinnamon and ginger. Any one of these can be omitted or reduced as each *chai-wala* has his own style. **Scott Griffiths, Canada**

1½ cups / 360 ml milk
½ cup / 120 ml water
small handful tea dust or 1-2 teabags
3 cardamom pods
4 whole cloves
small stick of cinnamon
2 pinches ginger
3 teaspoons sugar or to taste

1 First, crush the cardamom, cloves, and cinnamon in a mortar and pestle until fine.

2 Then combine the milk and water in a saucepan and heat over a high temperature.

3 Before the mixture is boiling, add the spice mix. As it begins to boil, put in the tea, ginger and sugar.

4 Let the tea froth up to the top of the pan, remove from heat and swirl for five seconds. Return to the heat and repeat three times. Strain into a cup and serve.

2 cups / 250 grams raw shelled peanuts *

FIRST MIX:
1 teaspoon salt
½ teaspoon freshly ground black pepper
½ teaspoon chili powder
1 teaspoon fine brown sugar (or to taste)

OR

SECOND MIX:
1 onion finely chopped
1 green chili, de-seeded and finely chopped
2 tablespoons cilantro/coriander, finely chopped
½ teaspoon chili powder
lemon or lime juice to taste
salt to taste

* Raw peanuts are available in most Asian and health food shops. If you have difficulty finding them, use unsalted, dry roasted peanuts. Just heat those through, instead of roasting them.

INDIA
Roast spicy peanuts ^V

PREPARATION AND COOKING: 10 MINUTES.

One of my earliest memories of street food is roasted, spiced peanuts. This snack was and still is a favorite all over India though it varies according to seasons, different nuts, regional tastes and available spices. My lasting memory comes from southern India especially on the coasts of Kerala and Chennai (Madras). After swimming in warm, blue seas my siblings and I nosed our way to the nearest peanut kiosk, where raw, shelled peanuts lightly laced in salt, pepper and chili (optional) with a faint touch of brown sugar, were carefully roasted inside a large earthenware pot shaped like a wok, over a wood fire.

Still sea-soaked, we'd dry out under the waning sun and watch the sunset while we crunched through aromatic, roasted peanuts carried in newspaper shaped into cones – or in folded banana leaves, which added their own delectable, fresh flavor. Some hawkers used cashews, chickpeas, lentils and other legumes but peanuts were the all-round favorite because they were cheaper, nutritious, delicious and very filling. **Leela Floyd, London, England**

1 Heat a heavy bottomed pan and turn the fire down low. Add peanuts and roast, stirring for about 8-10 minutes until done.
2 Season with the required amount of mix 1 and eat. For a more substantial version, mix roasted peanuts with the ingredients for mix 2, adding the lemon/lime juice at the end – serve while still warm.

Nariman Point chutney sandwiches

PREPARATION: 20 MINUTES

FOR THE GREEN CHUTNEY:
6 tablespoons mint leaves
3 tablespoons cilantro/coriander
2-3 green chilies, de-seeded and roughly chopped
juice of 1 lime
salt

OTHER INGREDIENTS – quantities dependent on how many sandwiches you are making:
bread, preferably white
butter
tomatoes, thinly sliced
cucumber, thinly sliced
potatoes, thinly sliced and boiled
salt

Nariman Point, on Mumbai's southern tip, is a cluster of pricey skyscrapers. Come lunch time and the *sandwich-walas* set up their tiny workstations to cater for the armies of office workers who descend to the pavements. The sandwiches are always made fresh on demand. White bread rules in India – but at least it has a good crumbly consistency, unlike Western supermarket bread. The sandwich-walas use butter liberally: it shows their customers that they don't stint on the quality of their ingredients.
The recipe below is the way these sandwiches are prepared in Mumbai. You can adapt it of course. Green chutney will keep for a few days in the fridge and is a great addition to other Indian street food recipes. **Dinyar Godrej, Rotterdam, Holland**

1 Put the mint, cilantro/coriander and chilies in a grinder or blender and process until they form a smooth paste. Stir in lime juice to taste and season with salt. The chutney should be tangy and hot. If you find it too fierce, add a little sugar.

2 To assemble the sandwiches, butter two slices of bread and spread each with half a teaspoonful of chutney. On one, add one layer each of the tomato, cucumber and potato slices and sprinkle with a little salt. Cover with the other slice. Using a sharp knife, cut off the crusts and slice diagonally to give you four small triangles. Make the rest in the same way.

INDIA
Ragda patties ^V

SERVES 4-5 AS A MAIN COURSE   PREPARATION: 15 MINUTES   COOKING: 45 MINUTES -1 HOUR

FOR THE RAGDA:

2 cans / 450 g canned chickpeas, drained
2 potatoes, cubed and boiled
1 tablespoon oil
1 teaspoon mustard seeds (preferably black)
8-10 curry leaves
¼ teaspoon asafetida *
½ teaspoon turmeric powder
1 teaspoon chili powder
1 teaspoon ginger, crushed to a paste
½ teaspoon garam masala
2 teaspoons brown sugar
1 tablespoon tamarind soaked in a little hot water or 1 teaspoon tamarind concentrate
salt
raw onion rings to garnish +

FOR THE PATTIES:

2 pounds / 1 kg potatoes
2 teaspoons cumin seeds
2 tablespoons cornstarch/flour
1 onion, finely chopped
1 teaspoon finely chopped ginger
2 green chilies, de-seeded and finely chopped
1½ cups / 200 g peas
2 tablespoons cilantro/coriander, chopped
juice of ½ a lime
oil
salt and pepper

+ optional
* Flavoring available from Asian stores

This is really two meals in one. You can make the crispy patties on their own and dish them up with ketchup. Or just cook up a batch of the sour and spicy chickpea *ragda* to have with bread rolls or rice. At streetside stalls a huge tureen of ragda is kept simmering while the cook fries fresh batches of patties on a griddle.

This is great party food. The ragda can be made a day ahead, and the patties can also be shaped in advance and kept in the fridge until you are ready to fry them. As an alternative filling you can use the green chutney from Nariman Point chutney sandwiches (p 48).

1 First, boil the potatoes, then drain and set aside. To make the ragda, heat the tablespoonful of oil and add the mustard seeds, curry leaves and asafetida. Throw in the ginger, turmeric and chili powder. Stir quickly and add the chickpeas with their liquid, the potatoes, sugar, garam masala, tamarind and salt to taste. Bring to a boil and mash lightly to thicken the sauce; simmer for a few more minutes.

2 For the patty filling, heat a tablespoon of oil and cook the onion, ginger and chilies for a few minutes until the onion softens. Add the peas, salt and pepper. Cover and cook on a low heat for 3 minutes. Add the cilantro/coriander and cook for a further minute or two until it is wilted. Take off heat, add the lime juice and crush the mix lightly with a fork.

3 Now take the drained potatoes and put them in a large bowl with the cumin seeds, cornstarch/flour and salt to taste. Using your hands, crush and knead the potatoes into a soft dough. If it feels too damp, add a little more cornstarch/flour. Divide the dough into about 14 balls.

4 Next, take each ball and flatten between your palms to make a saucer-sized round. Add a spoonful of the pea filling in the center and bring up the edges of the dough to close. Pat with your hands until you have a smooth patty. Lay on a plate and make the rest.

5 Heat enough oil to shallow-fry and cook the patties for 4-5 minutes on each side until browned and crisp. Do not stir them as this increases the chances of their breaking up. If cooking in batches, keep the cooked patties warm in a low oven.

6 Serve a couple of patties with a helping of the ragda topped with a few onion rings on the side.

Pani puri
(spicy filled puris) ^V

MAKES 4 SNACK-SIZE SERVINGS   PREPARATION: 20 MINUTES,
PLUS 1 HOUR IN FRIDGE   COOKING: 30-40 MINUTES

Also called *gol guppa*, these spicy, crunchy water bombs are the most surprising street food snack. As making the *puris* at home is somewhat demanding, people rush to specialist street vendors. Once at their favorite *pani puri* stall, the vendor lines them up in a row and hands them an empty metal plate. Then, working at lightning speed, the vendor cracks open puris, fills them with chutney and spicy water and pops them onto the plates. Just as quickly, the puris disappear into expectant mouths. When I left India, this was the street food I most craved – until I found out how to make them. In India, the puris now tend to be factory-made; and some Asian shops in the West also stock them. You can make the components of this dish in advance. If you can't find Pani Puri masala (sometimes called Gol Guppa masala), use Jal Jeera masala. If your puris get a bit tough with keeping, put them in the oven for five minutes to crisp up again. **Dinyar Godrej, Rotterdam, Holland**

FOR THE PURIS:
1 cup / 150 g fine semolina
1 tablespoon flour
5 to 6 tablespoons soda water
salt
oil

FOR THE TAMARIND CHUTNEY:
1 tablespoon tamarind paste
4 tablespoons brown sugar
pinch of asafetida *
1 teaspoon cumin powder
½ teaspoon red chili powder
salt

FOR THE *PAN* – this needs
to go in the fridge for
one hour when made:
Pani Puri masala or Jal Jeera
  masala
1 tablespoon cilantro/fresh
  coriander, finely chopped

* Flavoring, available from Asian stores.

1 To make the puris, first mix the semolina, flour, soda water and salt to taste. Knead to make a fairly stiff dough. Keep covered under a damp cloth for 10 minutes.

2 Now roll out the dough thinly on a lightly floured surface and cut into bite-sized circles using either a glass or a cookie cutter. Place on a platter and cover with the damp cloth; roll out the leftover dough again, until it is used up. You should have about 35 dough circles.

3 Heat oil for deep frying and slip the dough disks in a few at a time. Press down lightly to make them puff up. Cook for a couple of minutes, then turn over to cook the other side. Handle gently to avoid cracking. When done, drain well and allow to cool. They should be completely puffed up. They can be made in advance and stored in an airtight container.

4 To make the tamarind chutney, boil the tamarind paste in a cup of water. Add the sugar, asafetida, cumin, chili and salt to taste and let it simmer until it thickens; allow to cool.

5 Put a heaped tablespoon (or to taste) of Pani Puri or Jal Jeera masala with the cilantro/coriander, if using, in 2 cups/500 ml of water and stir well. Refrigerate for an hour or so to let the flavors blend.

6 To serve, put out puris with the tamarind chutney and spicy water (stir again). Give each person a plate and teaspoon. Take a puri, crack a small hole in the top with a finger. Put a little tamarind chutney in it and top up with the spicy water until it is full. Pop into your mouth immediately and enjoy the explosion.

Pav bhaji (vegetables with bread)

SERVES 4 AS A MAIN COURSE   PREPARATION: 15 MINUTES   COOKING: 35 MINUTES

This one-dish meal (*pav* means bread, *bhaji* vegetables) appeared on the streets of Mumbai probably no more than 20-odd years ago. It soon became all the rage and *pav bhaji* stalls have sprung up all over north India. A buttery and tangy gloop of vegetables, it has old and young alike licking their chops. It is prepared on huge griddles: butter sizzles, vegetables and spices are added and stirred with gusto. The bread is also toasted on the griddles. Vendors constantly rake at the cooking vegetables with iron spatulas with an almighty clatter designed to attract custom.

If you can't find pav bhaji masala, try another Indian spice mix designed for vegetables or even the ubiquitous supermarket curry powder. Black salt (also called *kala namak* or *sanchal*) is actually pinkish in color and has a sulfurous smell – no wonder Indian kids call it 'farty salt'. If you can't find it, try substituting *chaat masala* or just a mix of salt and black pepper.

2 tablespoons butter *
2 onions, chopped
1 green bell pepper, finely diced
4 cloves garlic, crushed
4 tomatoes, chopped
2 potatoes, boiled and crushed
1½ cups / 150 g cauliflower florets, chopped small
2 carrots, finely diced
½ cup /50 g peas
½ teaspoon turmeric
1 tablespoon pav bhaji masala
½ teaspoon black salt
8 soft white sandwich rolls or buns
extra butter for spreading *
1 tablespoon cilantro/coriander, chopped
salt

* It must be butter!

1 Melt butter in a large pan and cook the onion and bell pepper for a couple of minutes. Add garlic and cook for a further minute or two, until the onion softens.

2 Add tomatoes and cook at a brisk simmer until the butter begins to separate from the vegetables, about 10 minutes. While this is happening parboil the cauliflower, carrot and peas in a little water, for about 4 minutes, and drain, keeping the water.

3 Add all the spices to the tomato mixture and cook for a minute or two. Then add the boiled vegetables and the potato. Stir thoroughly and add a bit of the reserved water at a time until you have a thick broth-like consistency. Check seasoning and leave the bhaji on a low heat while you get the bread ready.

4 Heat a griddle or a heavy-bottomed frying pan. Slice each roll or bun in two horizontally and spread with a little butter. Place buttered side down on the griddle and dot the other side with a little butter too. When one side is crisp and lightly browned, turn and heat briefly on the other side.

5 Sprinkle the vegetables with chopped cilantro/coriander and serve with the hot bread.

Dahi vada (lentil cakes) Va

SERVES 4 AS A STARTER OR SIDE DISH   PREPARATION: 10 MINUTES   COOKING: 30 MINUTES PLUS OVERNIGHT SOAKING

These lentil cakes are a party favorite. When they were made at my parents' home, it was pointless cooking anything else as it would be left untouched. But as children we would also guiltily sneak out to buy them on the street with our pocket money.

It seems odd to fry something to a delectable crispness only to soak it in water. But the proof of the pudding is in the tasting. At a pinch you can soak the lentils an hour beforehand, rather than overnight, but the resultant *vadas* will be somewhat heavier. Use the skinned white urid lentils, rather than the ones with the black covering still on. The vadas can be fried, soaked and squeezed in advance and kept refrigerated until you need them. **Dinyar Godrej, Rotterdam, Holland**

1 cup / 200 g urid dal, soaked
1-2 green chilies, de-seeded
¼ teaspoon asafetida powder
1 teaspoon chopped ginger
oil
2 cups / 440 ml plain yogurt
1 teaspoon lightly roasted cumin
   powder
½ teaspoon garam masala
1 quantity tamarind chutney *
chaat masala +

* See p 53
+ optional

1 Drain the urid dal and put into a food processor with the chilies, asafetida, ginger and salt to taste. Grind thoroughly. Add a little water until you have a thick paste – it should drop easily from a spoon but not be so thin as to pour.

2 Heat the oil over a medium fire. Scoop a tablespoon of the mixture at a time and ease it into the oil with the aid of another tablespoon. The balls of batter will sink and then rise. Let them fry for 4-5 minutes on one side, until they are browned, and then turn over to brown the other side.

3 Drain on kitchen paper and then slip into a large bowl of water. Let them soak for 15 minutes.

4 Beat the yogurt with a little water into a pouring consistency. Add the roasted cumin powder, garam masala and salt to taste. Stir.

5 Take the soaked vadas and gently squeeze them flat with the palms of your hands. Place on a serving platter. Pour the seasoned yogurt over them.

6 Serve with tamarind chutney and top with a sprinkle of chaat masala, if you like.

INDONESIA

Chicken satay

SERVES 4   PREPARATION: 30 MINUTES (INCLUDING MARINATING TIME)   COOKING: 10 MINUTES

Satay – little kebabs of chicken, pork, beef and seafood – are found in Malaysia, Vietnam, Thailand; in fact throughout the whole region. In Indonesia it may be sold in the *warungs* (food stalls) or from the handcart called *kaki-lima* – 'five legs'– which are the three wheels of the cart and the two of the vendor. A favorite with Western visitors to southeast Asia, satay with peanut sauce is delicious and easy to recreate at home.

1½ pounds / 675 g chicken, cubed

MARINADE:
4 tablespoons soy sauce
4 tablespoons water
4 cloves garlic, crushed/minced
1 teaspoon sugar

PEANUT SAUCE:
1 onion, chopped
1-inch/2.5-cm piece fresh ginger, chopped
1 clove garlic, minced/crushed
1 teaspoon chili powder
1 tablespoon brown sugar
4 oz / 100 g raw peanuts, freshly fried or 4 oz crunchy peanut butter
¾ cup / 175 ml coconut milk
1 tablespoon lime or lemon juice
oil
salt

1 Start by making the marinade. Mix together the ingredients and pour over the chicken pieces in a bowl; leave for 30 minutes.

2 When ready, thread the meat onto skewers (small wooden ones if possible).

3 To make the peanut sauce, mix the onion, ginger, garlic, chili, sugar and peanuts or peanut butter in a blender, adding oil to make a smooth paste.

4 Heat some oil in a wok and cook the blended spice mix for 1 minute or so. Then spoon in the marinade juices and cook for a couple of minutes, stirring.

5 Now add enough coconut milk to achieve a thick but not solid sauce; keep warm. When you are ready, sprinkle in the lime juice and serve.

6 Cook the chicken over the barbecue or under a preheated broiler/grill and serve with the hot peanut sauce.

Nasi goreng (fried rice)

SERVES 4-6   PREPARATION: 10 MINUTES   COOKING: 5 MINUTES

As a first-time delegate at a meeting on sustainable development in Bali, I was feeling disheartened. It seemed that every agreement reached was being diluted by the addition of statements such as 'where appropriate' or 'where feasible' thus mitigating any feeling that the 'major players' were serious about addressing issues of inequality and justice.

It was therefore refreshing to walk on the beach at Nusa Dua and eat *nasi goreng*, cooked at a little mobile stall under the trees – an honest dish and enjoyed all the more in the company of very hospitable people, many of whom seemed to be so poor but were rich in hospitality and friendliness. I was sustained by both the food and their companionship. **Liz Cullen, County Kildare, Ireland**

½ pound / 225 g lean pork, sliced finely +
1 cup / 100 g shrimps or prawns, cooked +
1 cup / 225 g rice, cooked
2 eggs
1 onion or 4 shallots, chopped
1 red chili, de-seeded and chopped
1-2 cloves garlic, chopped
½ teaspoon dried shrimp paste +
4 scallions/spring onions, sliced thinly
2 cups / 100 g mushrooms, sliced
2 tablespoons soy sauce
2 tablespoons fresh cilantro/coriander, chopped
oil

+ optional

1 First, beat the eggs and pour them into hot oil, tilting the pan or wok so that the mixture spreads evenly. When it is browned at the edges, turn it over and cook the other side for a short time. Remove the omelet from the pan, cool slightly and then cut into thin strips; set aside.

2 Blend together the onion or shallots, chili, garlic and shrimp paste, if using. Heat some oil in a wok or pan and cook the spice paste for 30 seconds-1 minute.

3 After that, put in the scallions/spring onions, mushrooms and thin slices of pork, if using. Cook for 1-2 minutes before adding the shrimps or prawns.

4 Now scoop in the rice and sprinkle on the soy sauce. Cook for 2 minutes, stirring well to combine all the ingredients. Garnish with the omelet strips and cilantro/coriander.

Tofu with chilies ^V

SERVES 2   PREPARATION: 5 MINUTES   COOKING: 10 MINUTES

The absolute best food from a street stall that I ever had is very simple. I got addicted to it when living in Bali and went to the stall every night, particularly during my pregnancy! It's big deep-fried cubes of firm tofu, served with thick sweet soy sauce and then the chilies. **Charlotte Esser, Auckland, New Zealand/ Aotearoa**

½ pound / 225 g tofu, cut into cubes
soy sauce, in a small bowl
1-2 green chilies, de-seeded and chopped very finely or put a little chili powder into a small dish
oil

1 Heat the oil in a wok and when it is hot, put in the tofu cubes. Stir-fry briskly until they are golden brown all over. Remove the pieces and drain on absorbent paper.

2 Allow the tofu to cool a little. Pour some soy sauce into a bowl and place the chilies or chili powder in a little dish. Dip the tofu pieces in the soy sauce and then the chili.

Egg-plant/aubergine with coconut milk V

SERVES 4   PREPARATION: 10 MINUTES   COOKING: 10 MINUTES

The fifth most populous country in the world, Indonesia is made up of about 14,000 islands, including the original 'spice islands' that were the lure for Christopher Columbus' voyages in the 15th century.

2 pounds / 1 kg egg-plants/aubergines, cubed
2 tomatoes, chopped
1-2 chilies, de-seeded and finely chopped
1 onion or 3 shallots, sliced
3 cloves garlic, chopped
2 cups / 500 ml coconut milk
2 scallions/spring onions, chopped
salt

1 Put the egg-plant/aubergine cubes and tomatoes in a pan with the chilies, onion or shallots and garlic. Add enough water just to cover and simmer for 10 minutes or so, uncovered, until the egg-plant/aubergine is cooked.

2 Now stir in the coconut milk and season. Heat through gently and then serve, garnished with the chopped scallions/spring onions.

Food vendor, Jakarta, Indonesia.

Tempeh
(fermented soy bean cakes) Va

SERVES 4   PREPARATION: 10 MINUTES   COOKING: 15 MINUTES

2 blocks tempeh, cut into long
    thin strips
2-4 cloves garlic, minced/crushed
1-2 red chilies, de-seeded and sliced
1 teaspoon ground coriander
1 inch/2.5 cm galangal, sliced or
    use 1 teaspoon galangal powder +
½ teaspoon dried shrimp paste +
1-2 tablespoon soy sauce
1-2 teaspoon brown sugar
1 tablespoon cilantro/coriander,
    chopped
1 lime or lemon, cut into wedges
salt
oil

+ optional

This may be sold by the *pikulan* – the 'stick' sellers, similar to those in Thailand and other parts of southeast Asia, who carry their food in a basket at one end of a pole, with sometimes a cooking pot and utensils in the other basket. The pole is like a yoke carried on the shoulders with one hand to secure it. The vendor will happily sit down on the pavement and unbundle the goods for cooking. The dried shrimp paste is called *trasi* or *belacan* and is available in Chinese stores.

1 In a bowl, mix the garlic, chilies, coriander, galangal and shrimp paste, if using. Now pour in the soy sauce and sugar; season, and stir well to mix all the ingredients.

2 Heat some oil in a wok and when it is hot fry the tempeh slices until golden. Drain and set aside.

3 Next, heat the spice sauce, stirring well. Put the tempeh back in and turn the pieces around in the sauce.

4 Stir-fry for a few moments and then garnish with the cilantro/coriander. Serve with rice and the lime or lemon wedges.

Laksa stall, Penang, Malaysia.

Penang asam laksa (soup)

SERVES 4-6   PREPARATION: 20 MINUTES   COOKING: 10 MINUTES

1 onion, sliced

3 tablespoons laksa paste (see below) *

6 cups / 1.5 liters fish stock

1 teaspoon tamarind paste or juice of
    1 lime

½ pound / 225 g rice or laksa noodles

¼ pound / 110 g white fish or
    mackerel, filleted

1 cup / 100 g prawns

¾ cup / 75 g bean sprouts

2 tablespoons fresh or canned pineapple,
    cut into chunks

2 tablespoons cilantro/coriander, chopped

2 tablespoons mint

oil

salt

FOR THE PASTE –
makes 1½ cups / 375 g *:

1 cup / 100 g cooked prawns or shrimps

2-4 chilies, de-seeded and chopped

6-8 scallions/spring onions, chopped

6 cloves garlic, chopped

4-inch/10-cm piece fresh ginger,
    peeled and chopped

1 inch/2.5 cm galangal, sliced

2 teaspoons dried shrimp paste (belacan) *

2 stalks lemon grass, chopped

½ cup almonds

½ tablespoon turmeric

½ cup / 125 ml oil

* Ready-made Laksa paste and belacan can be
obtained in some Chinese or Asian stores.

I ate this several times in Penang – as one must! Mr Tong had a small stall at a café in bustling Air Itam, at the foot of Penang Hill. His soup was of course freshly made, topped with mint leaves. Later, near Pulau Tikus market, I sampled another version; same soup, different nuances.
William Beinart, Oxford, England

1 First make the paste by placing all the ingredients in a blender and process to a fine paste. Take out what is required for the recipe and transfer the rest into a screw-top jar to keep in the fridge.

2 For the soup, heat the oil and then add the onion and cook until soft. Stir in the laksa paste and mix well together for a couple of minutes. Now pour in the fish stock and tamarind paste or lime, increase the heat and simmer the soup for 10 minutes. Add half the cilantro/coriander.

3 While that is happening, place the noodles in a large bowl and pour over boiling water to cover them. Leave to stand for 3 minutes or until they are soft. Drain, and rinse noodles in hot water. (Or cook according to packet instructions).

4 Add the fish and prawns to the broth and simmer for 5 minutes or so until it is cooked.

5 Divide the cooked noodles among 4 bowls and spoon the soup over. Garnish with the bean sprouts, pineapple pieces, mint and remaining cilantro/coriander.

TROTH WELLS/NEW INTERNATIONALIST

Pacri nenas (pineapple curry) ^V

SERVES 4   PREPARATION: 10 MINUTES   COOKING: 15 MINUTES

Some of the best food stalls are near Fort Cornwallis on Penang's sea front. Every day, the stalls are packed with government workers – who usually have a nose for good food.

1 medium pineapple, cut into chunks, or use canned

1 star anise

1 stick cinnamon or 1 teaspoon powdered cinnamon

1 teaspoon cardamom seeds

2 cloves

1 teaspoon coriander seeds

2 scallions/spring onions, chopped

½ inch/1 cm ginger, grated, or ½ teaspoon powdered ginger

½ cup / 100 g candlenuts, macadamias or cashews, chopped

1 cup / 200 ml coconut milk

½ red chili, de-seeded and sliced finely

sugar +

water

oil

+ optional

1 First, make the spice paste by grinding together the star anise, cinnamon, cardamom, cloves and coriander.

2 Now heat some oil in a pan and sauté the scallions/spring onions, ginger and the nuts for 30 seconds or so over a high heat. Then lower the temperature and add the spice paste. Mix well and cook for a further minute.

3 When ready, put in the pineapple chunks and the coconut milk. Bring the dish slowly to the boil, stirring frequently. Add a little sugar if the pineapple is sour. Cook for 5-10 minutes until the pineapple is soft, adding more coconut milk or water to prevent sticking. Garnish with red chili and serve with rice.

Roti canai
(lentil dal and pancake) V

SERVES 4 PREPARATION (FOR DAL): 10 MINUTES
(FOR ROTI): 15 MINUTES PLUS 8 HOURS
COOKING (FOR DAL): 20 MINUTES (FOR ROTI): 5-10 MINUTES

A classic Malaysian hawker dish; delicious and worth having
just to enjoy watching the skill of the cook making the
pancakes, with a twist, a swirl and a flourish of thin dough
that is very hard to replicate. An easier version is below, but
the dough must sit for 8 hours or so. You can also serve the
dal with bought chapatis, puris or parathas. Use this curry
as filling for South African 'bunny chow' on p 25.

FOR THE DAL:
1 cup / 200 g red lentils or
   yellow split peas
1 teaspoon turmeric
1 egg-plant/aubergine, cubed
2 tomatoes, chopped
1 carrot, diced
1 potato, cubed
1 onion, chopped
1-2 chilies, de-seeded and
   finely chopped
1 cup / 200 ml coconut milk
½ cup / 110 ml water
½ teaspoon tamarind paste
1 teaspoon mustard seeds
1 teaspoon cumin seeds
1 sprig curry leaves
2 shallots or 1 small onion
   chopped
2-3 cloves garlic, chopped
salt
oil

FOR ROTI:
3 cups / 300 g flour
1 teaspoon salt
½ cup / 110 ml water
margarine

1 First, put lentils or peas into a pan with enough water to cover. Add the turmeric and then bring to the boil, removing the froth with a spoon. Simmer, covered, for 10 minutes.

2 Now add the egg-plant/aubergine, tomatoes, carrot, potato and onion. Continue to simmer until everything is cooked, and then put in half the chili. If the mixture becomes too dry during cooking, add a little more water.

3 When this is done, pour in the coconut milk, salt and tamarind. Mix well and cook gently for 5 minutes or so before turning off the heat.

4 Next, heat a little oil in a wok or pan and toast the mustard and cumin seeds until they begin to jump about. Put in the curry leaves, remaining chili, shallots or onion and garlic. Fry, stirring, until the onion or shallots and garlic are golden. Then turn this spice mix into the dal and stir well to combine.

5 Cover the pan and cook very gently for a few more minutes to heat through. Serve with hot chapatis, puris or parathas or make rotis (below).

6 For the roti, mix the ingredients in a bowl to make a smooth dough. Then make into golf-ball-size pieces and knead each one. Smooth on some margarine, using your hands. Place the dough balls back into the bowl and cover with a damp cloth. Leave for 8 hours or overnight.

7 When ready to cook, take a roti ball and roll it out on a lightly floured surface. Try to make it as thin as possible. When that is done, roll it up and, holding the roll vertically, flatten it down to make a circle.

8 Heat pan or griddle/skillet with a little oil and fry both sides until golden. To serve, hand round the hot rotis and put the curry into a bowl, or individual bowls. Break off bits of the bread and scoop out the curry (or use a spoon).

Char koay teow (flat rice noodles)

SERVES 4   PREPARATION: 15 MINUTES   COOKING: 20 MINUTES

½ pound / 225 g flat rice noodles (*koay teow*) *
1 cup / 100 g prawns
1-2 Chinese sausages, sliced finely *
3 tablespoons garlic chives or chives, chopped
3 cups / 150 g bean sprouts
2 eggs, beaten
1 cup / 100 g bak choy *
oil
water

FOR CHILI PASTE:
6 cloves garlic, chopped
1-2 red chilies, de-seeded, sliced, and soaked
1 teaspoon shrimp paste/ belacan +

SEASONING:
1 tablespoon dark soy sauce
1 tablespoon light soy sauce
1 teaspoon sesame oil
sugar
salt

* Available from Chinese stores.
+ optional

In downtown Georgetown, Penang, the Rio Hotel and Kedai Kopi (café) is built of Shanghai plaster that was fashionable before the War. Outside its characteristic yellow blinds, the *char koay teow* is being fried with great vigor. Mr Yeap Seng Cheng has been selling the dish since 1996. He works with an ingenious contraption with a handle... fixed to a fan. Rotating the handle with his left hand, he is able to regulate the heat of the fire while frying the noodles. Throwing prawns into his wok, he adds garlic, some *bak ewe p'ok* or dripping and then tosses in the *koay teow*. Next, cockles, Chinese sausages, chives and bean sprouts are added. The dish is finished off with egg and chili if desired. Its piquant aroma clouds that part of the street... **Penang Food Odyssey**

1 To begin, make the chili paste by grinding or blending the chili with the garlic and the shrimp paste/belacan, if using.

2 Heat the oil in a wok and gently fry the chili paste. Now increase the heat, put in the prawns and sausage; stir-fry for 1-2 minutes.

3 When ready, sprinkle in the seasoning sauce ingredients, plus the bean sprouts, bak choy, 2 tablespoons of the chives, and noodles. Stir vigorously to combine all the items, and add a little water to keep it moist.

4 Now spread out the mixture to the sides of the wok, making a space in the middle. Pour in the beaten egg and cook it there before distributing it among the noodles.

5 Continue to cook for a minute or two more, adding salt to taste and adjusting the seasonings as desired. Serve hot with remaining chopped chives on top.

Hainan-style chicken rice

SERVES 6   PREPARATION: 30 MINUTES   COOKING: 1-2 HOURS

One of the most popular hawker dishes. In Malaysia the glaze is often a rich red, made from a nice honey/ginger paste – delicious.

FOR THE CHICKEN:
3 pound/1.5 kg chicken
1-inch/2.5-cm piece of ginger, grated
2 cloves garlic
1-2 teaspoons honey
2 teaspoons sesame oil
2 teaspoons soy sauce
4 cups / 1 liter water or stock
salt and pepper

FOR THE RICE:
2 cups / 450 g rice
4 cloves garlic, crushed/minced
1-inch/2.5-cm piece of ginger, sliced
salt

FOR THE CHILI SAUCE:
½ red chili, de-seeded
2 cloves garlic
1-inch/2.5-cm piece of ginger, sliced
1 teaspoon salt
½-1 teaspoon sugar
juice of ½ lime or lemon

FOR THE SOUP:
2 cups / 100 g bean sprouts or
    cabbage, shredded

GARNISH:
1 cucumber, sliced
1 scallion/spring onion or
    1 tablespoon chives, chopped

Heat oven to 350°F/180°C/Gas 4 (see #2)

1 Start by making a chicken stock with the innards and the water. When done, keep about 3 cups/600 ml for cooking the rice in (see #3 below) and the remainder for the soup (see #4 below).

2 Prepare the chicken for roasting by making a paste of the ginger, garlic, honey, sesame oil, soy sauce, salt and pepper. Rub this over the chicken and set aside for 20 minutes. Now roast the chicken for an hour or more until cooked (see next step also). Allow to cool and then cut into slices. Set aside.

3 Towards the end of the chicken's cooking time, boil the rice in the chicken stock (see #1 above) with the garlic and ginger for 10 minutes or so, adding salt to taste.

4 While the rice is cooking, prepare the chili sauce by blending the ingredients together. Adjust the salt, sugar and lime juice. Put in a small dish. Make the soup by cooking up the remaining stock with the bean sprouts or cabbage, salt and pepper. Serve this in a separate bowl.

5 When ready, arrange the cucumber slices on a serving dish. Put the chicken in the middle, pouring over any juices, and garnish with scallion/spring onion or chives. Serve the rice, soup and chili sauce separately.

Nasi lemak
(coconut rice with sambal)

SERVES 4-6   PREPARATION: 20 MINUTES   COOKING: 20 MINUTES

To be home is to eat *nasi lemak* again! This popular breakfast dish is sold all over, often in attractive packets wrapped in banana leaves. The basic coconut rice is often supplemented with prawn *sambal*, hard-boiled eggs, cucumber slices, and *sambal ikan bilis*, a pungent mix including whitebait, chilies, fermented shrimp paste (*belacan*) and fried peanuts.

FOR THE RICE:
2 cups / 450 g rice
½ cup / 120 ml coconut milk
½ teaspoon ginger, finely chopped
1 pandanus leaf or a few drops of screwpine water +
water

+ optional

FOR THE PRAWN SAMBAL:
1½ cups / 300 g prawns
4 red chilies, de-seeded and chopped
½ teaspoon shrimp paste
4 shallots or 1 onion, sliced
1 teaspoon tamarind paste
oil
sugar
salt
water

OPTIONAL OTHER DISHES:
4 hard-boiled eggs, quartered
1 cucumber, sliced
Fried peanuts

1 Begin by cooking the rice in a pan with enough water to cover. Add the coconut milk, salt, ginger and screwpine or pandanus leaf. Bring to the boil and simmer gently until the rice is cooked, about 15 minutes. Set aside.

2 Make the sambal by first blending or grinding the chilies, shrimp paste, and shallots or onion. Make a smooth mixture, adding water as required.

3 Heat some oil in a wok and gently fry the paste for 1-2 minutes until it is fragrant.

4 Now add the prawns and stir-fry briskly for 3-5 minutes until they are cooked. Add the tamarind paste, salt and a little sugar to taste, if desired. Stir and continue to cook over a low heat.

5 Serve the rice on a plate with the prawn sambal and other condiments grouped around it.

Apam stall, Penang, Malaysia.

TROTH WELLS/NEW INTERNATIONALIST

Apam (pancakes)

MAKES 15   PREPARATION: 5 MINUTES   COOKING: 5 MINUTES

See the crowd round the apam-maker's stall? It's hard to resist these sweet mouthfuls. There are Chinese and Indian versions of these popular pancakes, usually made in a custom-built apam cooker, a griddle with little indentations.

3 cups / 300 g flour
4 teaspoons baking powder
3 teaspoons sugar
2 eggs, beaten
2 cups water
1 cup / 240 ml milk
2 tablespoons oil
salt

FILLING INGREDIENTS
– choose from:
toasted sesame seeds
roughly chopped
  peanuts
margarine and sugar
sweetcorn

1 In a bowl, sift together the flour, baking powder, sugar and a pinch of salt. Make a well in the middle and then pour in the eggs, water, milk and oil. Beat to make a smooth batter.

2 Now heat a little oil in a small frying pan. Let it get hot and when it is ready, pour in a tablespoon of batter and spread it evenly. When the edges are crisp, spoon the desired filling on to the pancake.

3 Continue to cook, covered, for a further couple of minutes. Fold the pancake over before serving. Repeat to use up all the mixture.

Sambal kangkong (stir-fried spicy greens)

SERVES 4   PREPARATION: 5 MINUTES   COOKING: 5 MINUTES

A Nonya ('Straits Chinese') speciality, and very tasty of course. *Kangkong*, also called water convolvulus, is a green vegetable found in most Malaysian markets. You can find it outside the country in Chinese stores. This dish can be served with prawns.

2 pounds / 1 kg kangkong greens, chopped *
1-2 red chilies, de-seeded and finely chopped
4 cloves garlic, chopped
½ teaspoon shrimp paste
1 tablespoon soy sauce
oil
salt
water

* Available in Chinese stores. If you cannot obtain it, use fresh spinach.

1 Heat the oil in a wok and sauté the chilies (keeping a few slices for garnish), garlic and shrimp paste, for a few minutes until the flavors are released and they are combined into a paste.

2 Add the kangkong, a little water, salt and soy sauce. Toss well with the paste and cook until the leaves are soft. Garnish with red chili slices.

亞參叻沙
ASAM LAKSA
炒粿條
CHAR KOAY TEOW
蝦麵
PRAWN MEE
豬腸粉
CHEE CHEONG FUN
炒豬腸粉
CHAR CHEE CHEONG FUN

TROTH WELLS/NEW INTERNATIONALIST

Food signs, Malaysia.

Seekh kebabs

MAKES 12   PREPARATION: 10-20 MINUTES PLUS 1 HOUR STANDING TIME   COOKING: 10 MINUTES

A Punjabi recipe widely eaten in both the Pakistani and Indian Punjab regions. In Jhelum, Pakistan, groups of young men would gather at street-side restaurants in the hot evenings to eat *seekh kebabs* together. The kebabs are often served with naan bread, sliced cucumber and lettuce and, importantly, yogurt (*dhai*) and mint chutney (*podina*) or *raita* (see p 81), drizzled with fresh lemon juice. Tastes tangy, juicy and very more-ish. **Imran Mirza, Oxford, England**

1 pound / 450 g minced mutton or lamb *
1 onion, finely chopped *
1-3 green chilies, de-seeded and finely chopped *
1½ teaspoons garam masala
1 tablespoon gram (chick-pea) flour
1 teaspoon cumin seeds
3 scallions/spring onions, finely chopped
1-2 tablespoons mint, finely chopped
1-2 tablespoons cilantro/coriander, finely chopped
1-2 lemons, cut into wedges
salt

* At most Pakistani butchers', when buying minced mutton, it is quite common to ask for onion and chilies to be put through the mincer at the same time as the meat, and for the whole ensemble to go through it twice.

1 Once the onion and chilies have been either minced with the meat or finely chopped and added to it in a large bowl, sprinkle in the garam masala and the cumin, kneading all the while. Then add the gram flour, mint, cilantro/coriander and salt.

2 With one hand, hold the edge of the bowl and with the other just squelch and squash the ingredients. Swivel the bowl round a little and squelch again. Continue to do this for a few minutes, to combine everything. Cover the bowl and leave in the fridge for an hour or so. This might be a good time to prepare the chutney or raita (see p 81).

3 When ready to cook, take a skewer and, regularly dipping your hand in a bowl of cold water (to prevent the mixture sticking to your hand rather than the skewer), take a handful of mixture and pack it on, squeezing up and down the length of the skewer. The kebab should be 5-7 inches/12-15 cm in length.

4 Cook under a medium-hot grill or over a barbecue, turning regularly, until slightly charred on the ends and cooked through. Squeeze lemon juice over before eating.

Cooking seekh kebabs, Pakistan.

Flat bread ^V

MAKES 12   PREPARATION: 20 MINUTES PLUS RESTING TIME 1 HOUR   COOKING: 5 MINUTES

Anyone who has visited Pakistan will remember the marvelous unleavened bread freshly baked in all street stalls and cafés there. Back home I experimented to try and obtain a taste close to the original (which would require a special brick oven to whose side the bread is stuck until it cooks) in an ordinary city kitchen. The result is surprisingly true to the original. This bread is a traditional accompaniment for kebab dishes or dal, and is a popular breakfast with travelers (plain, with butter and/or honey). Back home, it is also an excellent alternative wrap for your sandwich meals, or – if prepared in advance and frozen – a great solution for those evenings when you get home too late and too tired to cook anything: just put it in a pan for a couple of minutes with tomato sauce, cheese, olives and so on for a ready-in-a-minute pizza, or fill with whatever else takes your fancy.

Street food is still popular in Italy, especially in harbor towns like Genoa, but each day we risk seeing them wiped out by some 'hygiene' EU regulation. Many of the dishes are made from really sustainable ingredients (like the wonderful array of chickpea flour snacks traditional in my region). **Laura Parodi, Genoa, Italy**

3½ cups / 340 g durum wheat flour
2 cups / 200 g wholemeal flour
1-2 tablespoons oil
1 teaspoon salt

1 Combine all the ingredients in a bowl, adding just as much water as required to make a soft but consistent dough. Cover the bowl with a damp cloth and set aside for 1 hour.

2 After that, cut egg-sized pieces and roll out each one on a floured surface, to roughly 12 inches/30 cm in diameter.

3 Put a little oil in a large frying pan and then lower each piece of bread into the pan and cook it while you roll out the next one. After a short time, a few bubbles will appear on top, showing that it is ready. If you want to be able to freeze or re-heat it, only cook on one side. Take it out (using tongs if that helps).

4 Cook all the breads in the same way. If you wish to freeze them, turn off the heat before returning them all to the frying pan. Cover it with a lid and leave to cool; then freeze.

Mint and yogurt chutney or raita ^{Va}

SERVES 4   PREPARATION: 5 MINUTES

This can be prepared while the ingredients for the main dish, such as kebabs (p 78), are marinating.

Street stall, Pakistan.

3-4 tablespoons mint
¼-½ green chili, de-seeded
**   and chopped**
1 cup / 240 ml set yogurt
a few pomegranate seeds +
salt

+ optional

1 Put the mint, chili, pomegranate seeds, if using, and the salt into a blender or large mortar and make a purée.

2 Add the yogurt and stir well to integrate the mix. Add more yogurt or a little milk if necessary to make the desired consistency.

Tom yam (hot and sour soup)

SERVES 4   PREPARATION: 10 MINUTES   COOKING: 10 MINUTES

½ pound / 225 g prawns *

6 cups / 1.5 liters chicken or fish stock

2 stalks lemongrass, cut in half

4 lime leaves, torn ** +

1 onion or 3 shallots, chopped

3 cloves garlic, chopped

2 tomatoes, chopped

2-inch/5-cm piece of fresh galangal, cut into thick slices or 2 teaspoons galangal powder

½ pound / 225 g mushrooms, halved

2-4 green chilies, de-seeded and cut in half lengthwise

3 tablespoons fish sauce

2 tablespoons lime or lemon juice

3-4 tablespoons cilantro/ coriander, chopped

* If using unpeeled prawns, peel them and keep the peelings for stock.
** Obtainable in Chinese/Asian stores. Or use a little lime peel.
+ optional

A delicious hot, fragrant, spicy soup, flavored with lime and chili – far removed from *kaeng jeut* (bland soup, see p 85), a milder broth with noodles, tofu and Chinese radish. You can of course use more chilies, but see how it tastes to you. If you want to reduce their spiciness, leave the chilies whole instead of cutting them. **Colin Jennings, County Armagh, Northern Ireland**

1 If using prawn peelings for the stock, discard them when ready to start the soup.

2 Put in the lemon grass, kaffir lime leaves, onion or shallots, garlic, tomatoes and galangal into the stock. Bring it back to the boil and then simmer, covered, for about 3 minutes.

3 Now add the mushrooms, chilies and fish sauce. Cook gently for 2 minutes before putting in the prawns. Bring back to the boil and cook the prawns. When they are ready, turn off the heat and remove the lemon grass. Pour in the lime or lemon juice and scatter in half the cilantro/ coriander. Stir well.

4 Garnish with the remaining cilantro/coriander and serve with a bowl of plain boiled rice.

Minced spicy chicken or pork salad

SERVES 2-4   PREPARATION: 15 MINUTES   COOKING: 20 MINUTES

I got to know about this dish when I worked with a nice old lady I met in Thailand. She asked me to eat at her stall one night, and I declined, saying I'd be back the next day. I kept my promise, which shocked her, and we started talking a little, with gestures and bits of each other's language. She agreed to let me work on her street stall in Sukothai. I got the recipe from her.' **Colin Jennings, County Armagh, Northern Ireland**

1 cup / 225 g minced chicken or pork
1½ tablespoons fish sauce
2 tablespoons lime juice
1 scallion/spring onion, sliced
2 shallots, sliced
½ teaspoon chili powder
1 tablespoon cilantro/coriander, finely chopped
5 mint leaves, chopped, plus a few leaves for garnish
½ cup / 120 ml water or stock

Vendor's cart, Thailand.

1 Pour the stock into a pan and bring it to the boil. When it is boiling, put in the minced meat, and stir until cooked.

2 Stir in the fish sauce and lime juice. Add the scallion/spring onion, shallots, chili, cilantro/coriander, mint leaves, and mix it all together.

3 Put on a serving plate or bowl and garnish with vegetables and mint leaves.

Kaeng jeut wun sen (mung bean noodle soup)

SERVES 4 PREPARATION: 10 MINUTES COOKING: 15 MINUTES

Quite the opposite from *tom yam* (p 83) is *kaeng jeut* (soothing or bland soup), with fish sauce and black pepper; common ingredients are *wun sen mung* bean noodles, *tao-huu* (tofu), *hua chai thao* (Chinese radish) and *muu sap* (ground pork).

In Thailand we often ate nourishing soup filled with noodles and vegetables, and meat if you wanted. A large cauldron of broth was kept hot and added to a selection of chopped vegetables, pork, chicken, fish or beef, sometimes tofu or noodles that were displayed in glass cabinets. You could choose your vegetables and the amount for your bowl. Chilies were also options. Instant; delicious. **Diana Grant-Mackie, Auckland, New Zealand/Aotearoa**

1 cup / 50 g mushrooms, sliced
1 cup / 225 g minced pork
½ cup / 75 g soft tofu, cut into cubes
2 cloves garlic, minced/crushed
1 teaspoon black pepper
4 cups / 1 liter chicken stock or water
½ cup / 50 g soaked mung bean noodles, cut into short lengths

4 cilantro/coriander roots or use 3 tablespoons leaves
⅓ cup lily buds +
2 tablespoons fish sauce
oil
salt

+ optional – or use bean sprouts.

1 Using a pestle and mortar or blender, grind the coriander root or leaves with the garlic and black pepper to make a paste.

2 Heat some oil in a pan and fry the pounded mix until fragrant. Then put in the pork and stir-fry over a medium heat till cooked.

3 When that is done, pour in the chicken stock and bring to the boil. Lower the heat, add the remaining ingredients and simmer for a few minutes.

PAUL BEINSSEN/LPI

Pad Thai (Thai noodles)

SERVES 6-8   PREPARATION: 5 MINUTES   COOKING: 15 MINUTES

Pad Thai, Thailand's signature dish, has several regional variations. As always, check the type of chili you are using and use less if you are in doubt as to its strength. It's easy to add more...

8 oz / 225 g vermicelli/thin rice noodles

1 cup / 150 g tofu, diced

1 cup / 100 g cooked prawns

½ red bell pepper, sliced

½ green bell pepper, sliced

2 scallions/spring onions, sliced

2 tablespoons fish sauce

5-6 cloves garlic, finely chopped

1-2 red chilies, de-seeded and finely sliced

1 cup / 50 g bean sprouts

juice of 2 limes

2 limes, cut into wedges

½ cup / 60 g roasted peanuts, coarsely chopped

2 tablespoons cilantro/coriander, chopped

sugar

1 Cook the vermicelli according to the packet instructions.

2 While they are soaking, heat a little cooking oil in a wok and cook the tofu pieces until they are golden. Then add the prawns and cook for a couple of minutes.

3 Next, put in the bell peppers, scallions/spring onions, fish sauce, garlic and chili. Stir round to amalgamate the ingredients, and cook for a further minute or two.

4 When that is done, add the drained noodles and pour in the lime juice. If desired, add a little sugar to taste.

5 Finally, toss in the bean sprouts and cook for another minute. Remove from the pan to a serving plate. Garnish with the lime wedges around the plate and scatter peanuts and cilantro/coriander on top.

Pho (beef noodle soup)

FOR 6-8 SERVINGS   PREPARATION: 20 MINUTES   COOKING: 1-2 HOURS (INCLUDING STOCK)

FOR THE SOUP:
2 pounds /1 kg beef bones or chopped oxtail
1 pound / 450 g beef brisket
2.5 quarts / 2.5 liters water
1 inch/2.5 cm piece of ginger, sliced
1 onion, chopped
3 whole star anise
3 whole cloves
1 cinnamon stick
1 cup / 200 g Chinese radishes cut into chunks
2 tablespoons fish sauce *
2 cups / 300 g flat rice noodles
½ pound / 225 g beefsteak, very thinly sliced
2 spring onions, finely sliced
2 limes, cut into wedges
salt and pepper

DIPPING SAUCE:
2 tablespoons fish sauce *
1 tablespoon lime juice
1 clove garlic, crushed
1-2 red chilies, de-seeded and finely chopped
1 teaspoon rice vinegar
1 teaspoon sugar

GARNISH:
1 cup / 100 g bean sprouts
6-8 lettuce leaves, chopped coarsely
2-3 tablespoons cilantro/coriander, chopped
1 tablespoon mint, chopped

* The Vietnamese variety is called *nuoc mam*.
You can use soy sauce instead

Wherever you go in Vietnam, from the busy side streets you stroll along in Hanoi to the mountain villages you stop at on your Minsk* motorbike, there will always be a place to buy a hot, nourishing and tasty *pho bo*. Served with draft beer, a huge side plate of greenery and a warm smile this is *the* fast food of Vietnam. **Jackie McAvoy, Tunisia**

*For those wondering, yes – it does really mean Minsk as in Belarus, formerly Soviet Union. There is a Hanoi Minsk Club with its own web page... which says 'You will not see many of these bikes in Hanoi as the locals consider themselves above such an ungainly, oil-billowing reminder of past Russian dominance. In the mountains and hills, however, the Minsk rules supreme.'

1 Place the water, bones and brisket in a deep pan and bring to the boil. While that is happening, grill or dry-fry the ginger and onion until they are almost burnt. Add them to the stock, plus the star anise, cloves, cinnamon and radishes.

2 Partially cover and simmer for 1½ hours, skimming frequently. Leave to cool and skim again, then add the fish sauce and seasoning and stir well. Drain the stock and retain it. Discard the other components, except the meat. Take this out and slice very finely.

3 Blanche the rice noodles in boiling water to soften and then divide them between 6 soup bowls. Put in the sliced cooked beef plus the raw beef which has been sliced paper-thin.

4 In a salad bowl add the bean sprouts, lettuce, mint and cilantro/coriander and mix lightly. Mix all the dipping sauce ingredients together and place in 4 small bowls.

5 When ready to serve, heat up the stock until boiling and pour it over the noodles and meat. Sprinkle with chopped scallions/spring onions and hand round the lime wedges. Eat using chopsticks and a spoon. Sprinkle occasionally with the garnish and dip the meat into the sauce.

Banh xeo (filled omelet/crepe)

SERVES 4-6   PREPARATION: 5 MINUTES   COOKING: 10 MINUTES

2 scallions/spring onions, chopped

2 cloves garlic, chopped

½ pound / 225 g minced pork

2 cups / 100 g bean sprouts

½ cup / 125 g prawns *

6 eggs

1-2 tablespoons cilantro/ coriander, chopped

1 tablespoon basil, chopped

1 tablespoon mint, chopped

1 tablespoon fish sauce **

8-12 lettuce leaves or as required

oil

salt

* Or use frozen/cooked prawns – see #2.
** *Nuoc mam*, Vietnamese fish sauce is widely available. You can use Thai fish sauce, *Nam pla*, soy sauce, or omit altogether.

Banh is a catch-all phrase for a wealth of snacks, baguettes, cakes, cookies and other delicious treats found in Vietnam. These are usually small items, and normally wrapped in some way, whether with an omelet or crepe as in this recipe, or carefully cosseted in banana leaves and tied firmly like a parcel. Wrapping the ingredients and then grilling over a wood or charcoal fire is one of the oldest forms of cooking. There are regional and ethnic specialties: yams, sweetcorn, cassava and rice are all frequently used. *Banh xeo* is made with pork and prawns, but you can replace these with vegetables such as mushrooms.

Hawker takes a break beneath mural, Hanoi, Vietnam.

CHRIS STOWERS/PANOS

1 Using a wok or frying pan, heat the oil and then sauté the scallions/spring onions for a few minutes before adding the garlic.

2 When they are soft, put in the pork mince and prawns; stir-fry it until the pork is brown and the shrimps are pink. If using cooked prawns, put them in once the pork is ready.

3 Next, add the bean sprouts and cook for a couple of minutes. Then put in half the cilantro/coriander. Add a little fish sauce or soy sauce and salt as necessary. Stir well and continue to cook for a further minute or so to combine all the ingredients. When done, turn off the heat, cover the wok or pan and keep warm.

4 Whisk the eggs. Heat some oil in a pan or wok and pour in the eggs, turning the pan so that they distribute. Flip or turn the omelet to cook the other side. When ready, spoon in the filling and add the remaining herbs before serving, garnished with lettuce leaves.

Mi bun xao voi rau dau (stir-fried vegetables) Va

SERVES 4   PREPARATION: 5 MINUTES   COOKING: 5-8 MINUTES

Pleasant, and if you have had enough of chilies this is not too hot.

4 oz / 100 g rice vermicelli *
2 cloves garlic, minced
1 carrot, finely sliced
¼ cup / 50 ml water or stock
1 cup / 50 g bak choi/Chinese
    cabbage,sliced
1 stick celery, or ½ bell pepper,
    sliced very finely
1 tablespoon oyster sauce +
1 tablespoon fish sauce or
    1 tablespoon light soy sauce
1 teaspoon sugar
1 tablespoon cilantro/coriander,
    chopped
pepper
oil

* Cooked according to packet
instructions.
+ optional

1 Heat the oil in a wok or pan over a high heat and fry the garlic and carrot for 30 seconds-1 minute.

2 Add the remaining ingredients, except the vermicelli, and stir to cook for 5 minutes, until the liquid has reduced a little.

3 Then toss in the drained vermicelli and mix well to combine. Serve immediately with the cilantro/coriander scattered on top as a garnish.

Com chien (fried rice)

SERVES 4-6   PREPARATION: 15 MINUTES   COOKING: 20 MINUTES

3½ cups / 450 g cooked rice
½ pound / 225 g prawns
1 onion, sliced finely
2 cloves garlic, crushed
2 tomatoes, sliced
2 scallions/spring onions, sliced
2 tablespoons cilantro/coriander, chopped
1 tablespoon fish sauce +
oil
salt and pepper

+ optional

A common sight on the streets in Vietnam is the *don ganh* carrier – nearly always a woman – bearing a bamboo pole as a yoke across her shoulders, with a basket containing food and/or utensils hanging from each end. If you hail her, she will come across. Sometimes, one basket contains a pot of soup cooking on a little portable burner; the vendor ladles it out into bowls for you. Other times she could unwrap a basket of spring rolls, *bành* (snacks, often wrapped in banana leaves), fruit or baguettes. Rice such as *com chien* is a common dish. This can be made in advance and frozen.

1 Heat the oil in a wok or pan and when it is hot, sauté the onion for a few minutes until it is transparent. Then put in the garlic and prawns and stir-fry for a few minutes.

2 After this, put in the tomatoes, the scallions/spring onions, and half the cilantro/coriander. Stir these around for a while before adding the cooked rice, and gently cook over a medium heat for 15-20 minutes, stirring frequently.

3 When ready, add the fish sauce if using, and seasoning. Mix well and serve topped with the remaining cilantro/coriander scattered on top.

Canh rau
(mixed vegetable broth) Va

6 SERVINGS   PREPARATION: 15 MINUTES   COOKING: 20 MINUTES

Vietnam's hawkers (usually men) push their carts up and down the streets selling sliced or chopped fruit – pieces of mango, pineapple, banana or papaya (paw-paw). He may offer you cooling sugar-cane juice, or lop the top off a fresh coconut, stick in a straw, and hand you a refreshing drink.

His friend's cart could be selling soup such as this one.

5 cups / 1.2 liters stock
1 cup / 100 g mixed vegetables, such as turnips, cauliflower, carrots, cabbage, finely chopped
1 cup / 50 g mushrooms, sliced
½ chili, de-seeded and finely chopped
2 scallions/spring onions, finely chopped
2 tablespoons cilantro/coriander, chopped
1 teaspoon fish sauce +
salt and pepper

+ optional

1 Heat the stock and add the vegetables, mushrooms, chili, one scallion/spring onion and half the cilantro/coriander. Simmer for 15 minutes or until they are all cooked. The longer it cooks, the more the flavors can develop.
2 Season; add the fish sauce if using, and scatter the remaining scallion/spring onion and cilantro/coriander on top before serving.

LATIN AM
& CA

Musicians at Havana Club
rum distillery, Havana, Cuba.

ERICA
RIBBEAN

para sentirse feliz

Imperial Ruso (Russian sandwich)

MAKES 2 SANDWICHES   PREPARATION: 5 MINUTES

This was apparently created by Cayetano Brenna, an Italian pastrycook, in 1917 to show solidarity with the Tsarist dynasty when the Bolsheviks stormed the Winter Palace – hence the name.

The sandwich is an important option for working people because they can buy it easily on their way to work. It is a typical food in the province of Salta. Basically, an *imperial* is a triple sandwich, with fresh-sliced tomato in one section, and thin pieces of roast meat in the other. Sometimes, the tomato is replaced or joined by lettuce. The *imperial ruso* can easily be carried or slipped into a bag or pocket. This is one of the reasons why they are so popular. They are sold almost everywhere: bars, restaurants, places where there are grills, bakeries – but also in kiosks, department stores, big supermarkets, photocopy stores, haberdashers', in stores in parking lots – well, everywhere!

One important characteristic is the way the vendor carefully wraps the sandwich in paper before giving it to you. **Jose Elosegui, Montevideo, Uruguay**

2 slices cooked meat
1 tomato
2 lettuce leaves
6 slices bread
butter or margarine
salsa +
salt and pepper +

+ optional

Butter 3 pieces of bread for each sandwich. Place the meat between 2 slices and the tomato and lettuce in the other section. Season and add salsa sauce or chutney if desired.

Tacqueria sign, Chicago, USA.

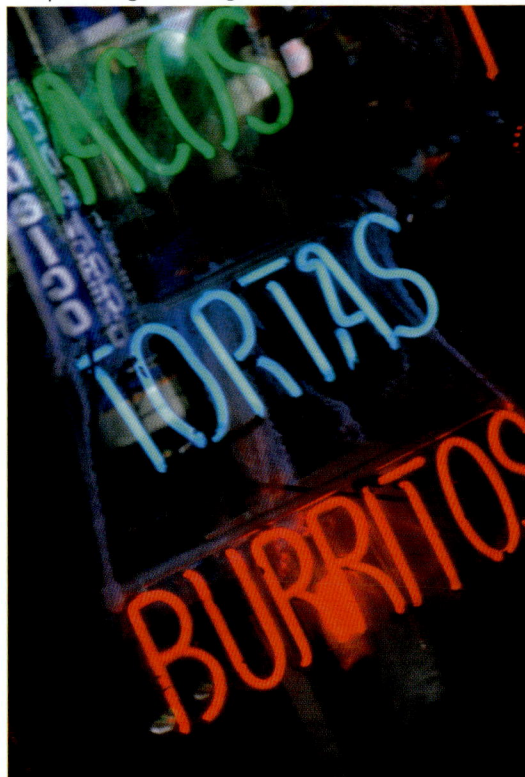

RAY LASKOWITZ/LPI

ARGENTINA

Sandwiche de Milanesa (breaded steak sandwich)

MAKES 4   PREPARATION: 5 MINUTES   COOKING: 10 MINUTES

The *milanesa* (steak) is put between two pieces of bread and that is the *sandwiche de milanesa*. It is favorite in Argentina. The same food is also eaten in Uruguay but with the name *milanesa al pan*. However, it is not very common to see Uruguayan people eating it in the streets, as happens in Argentina.

The origins of the 'Milanesa' name seem to lie in the troubled times of the 19th century when the Austrian Hapsburgs ruled part of Italy. The Austrian Marshal Radetzky apparently provided conclusive evidence in a letter when he wrote about discovering the *cotoletta* (chop or cutlet) *'alla milanesa'* and gave a careful description.

Workers often eat *sandwiches de milanesa* as lunch because they can be readily bought and eaten – important if you need to get back to work quickly. **Jose Elosegui, Montevideo, Uruguay**

4 thin steaks
1 cup / 100 g soft breadcrumbs
1-2 eggs
2 cloves garlic, chopped
2 tablespoons parsley, chopped
bread
oil
salt and pepper

1 Tenderize the steaks by hitting both sides with the end of a rolling pin. Then season.

2 Beat the eggs in a bowl. Now add the garlic, the parsley, and a bit of salt and pepper.

3 Take a large, rectangular dish and place half the breadcrumbs in it. Taking the steaks, dip them first into the bowl containing the egg mix and then into the dish with the breadcrumbs. Ensure they are well coated; repeat with all the pieces.

4 Heat the oil in a frying pan and when it is very hot, fry both sides of the steak. The milanesa is ready when both sides of the steak are browned. Serve hot in a bread sandwich.

Street food   97

Empanadas criollas (pasties) Va

SERVES 4-6   PREPARATION: 20 MINUTES   COOKING: 15-20 MINUTES

Every year in the Argentinean province of Tucumán, people celebrate the National Empanadas festival. In that province the local recipe contains meat, olives and raisins.

Empanadas are a good option for fast lunch and dinner. You can buy this food in every street market, especially in Tucumán's city centers where there are lots of offices and shops. Every province in Argentina has its own recipes, preparing sweet or savory empanadas. This food can be served with a variety of fillings – in this recipe you can substitute cooked beans for the meat.

Empanadas have a privileged place in popular food – in the countryside and in the cities. They are found at all kinds of parties and events.

½ **pound / 225 g frozen pastry, thawed**
½ **pound / 225 g ground/minced beef,
    or use cooked beans**
6 **scallions/spring onions, sliced thinly**
½ **cup / 60 g sultanas or raisins**
2 **teaspoons oregano**
½ **teaspoon cayenne pepper**
1 **teaspoon cumin**
1 **teaspoon paprika**
2 **roasted red pimientos, diced ***
10 **green olives, pitted**
3 **hardboiled eggs, sliced**
salt

* These are the long, tapering paprika peppers. You could use bell peppers instead.

1 In a large skillet, heat the oil. Partially mash the beans, if using. Add the meat or beans and half the scallions/spring onions. Sauté until they get slightly browned.

2 Now put in the sultanas or raisins and spices and cook until the meat is cooked through (or the beans hot). Stir in the remaining scallion/spring onion slices and roasted peppers. Let the mixture cool. Add a little water as necessary to make a moist mixture.

3 Roll out the pastry and cut with a saucer into circles. Fill one half of the empanada discs with meat, add 1 olive and 1 slice of egg. Fold over to form a semi-circle and seal the empanada, pressing the edges with a fork.

4 Preheat oil in a deep-fryer or wok. Cook the empanadas for about 3 minutes. Remove with a slotted spoon and drain on paper towels. Alternatively, if you do not want to fry, you can place them on a baking tray in a pre-heated oven (400°F/200°C/Gas 6) for 10-20 minutes until golden.

Yerba mate ^V

SERVES 4   PREPARATION: 5 MINUTES

Mate is a type of tea drunk all over South America; people with their thermos of hot water and *mate* are a common sight. It is traditionally drunk with friends and passed around in a circle, endlessly refilled. There is a cup, usually wooden or metal, filled with *yerba*, a concoction of crushed herbal leaves.

To drink, you use a wooden or metal straw (*bombilla*); the end that is in the cup has a filter at the bottom to keep the *yerba* leaves from coming into your mouth. You fill the cup with hot water to the top each time, but since it is packed with *yerba*, you can only have a couple of sips at a time. There are some strict rules. First, it is a huge insult to touch the *bombilla* with your hand, so you just grab the cup and drink without touching it. Always pass it around the circle and never drink twice in a row. When you have your last drink, say 'gracias', which tells the others that you are done, so that the next time it comes around you will be skipped. Most Argentineans add sugar each time, although I prefer it without sugar, with its dry, almost bitter, natural taste. It helps give you a little bit of motivation on a rainy day, although it's fine to drink any time. **Jose Elosegui, Montevideo, Uruguay**

The tea, bowls and bombillas are all available from websites on the internet, such as yerbamate.co.uk, and you can buy the tea in health food shops.

1 Put enough yerba into the bowl to come about three-quarters of the way up.

2 Heat water in a kettle and when it is warm, add a few drops to the tea to soak it.

3 When the water is hot but not boiling, pour more in to dampen all the tea. When the yerba is soaked, insert the bombilla and then top up the bowl with more hot water.

4 In case any bits have entered the bombilla, suck through it and discard any yerba powder. Add sugar to taste, if desired.

Wooden bowls for mate, Buenos Aires, Argentina.

KRZYSZTOF DYDYNSKI/LPI

Pasteis fritos (fried pies)

MAKES 12   PREPARATION: 20 MINUTES PLUS 1 HOUR SET ASIDE   COOKING: 20 MINUTES

Popular foods, like *cachorro-quente* (hot dog), *pipoca* (popcorn), and *bauru* (steak sandwich), are not sold everywhere in Brazilian cities. You will not find people selling these foods in the richest neighborhoods, but you will in the poorest and middle-class ones. On the beaches the situation is different. They seem to be more democratic and people of all social classes get together there, so the sellers walk along the beaches and promenades offering foods, mainly *milho cozido* (boiled sweetcorn). This popular food is eaten at the seaside all over Brazil. The *pasteis* are quite big and can be filled with meat, egg, olives, chicken, or – usually on the beach – fish. On the beaches there are also vendors with baskets offering *pasteis de siri* (crabs), *pasteis* with prawn, with chicken and other fillings.

Pastry shops frequently use the same fillings (chicken, beef, seafood, vegetables or cheese) to make small tartlets (*empadas*) which are also served as appetizers. *Pasteis* generally are filled with mixtures of meat , chicken or cheese. They are best served hot immediately after cooking.

FOR THE DOUGH:
1 cup / 100 g flour
1 tablespoon margarine
salt
½ beaten egg
water

FOR THE FILLING:
¼ pound / 110 g cheese, grated
1 onion, sliced finely
2 tablespoons fresh parsley, chopped finely
2 tablespoons tomato sauce or purée
1 hardboiled egg, chopped
6 olives, pitted and chopped
pepper sauce
oil
salt and pepper

1 Sift the flour and salt together into a bowl. Add the rest of the ingredients and a little water.

2 Mix well with the fingertips, adding a few more drops of water if the dough seems dry. Cover with plastic film and set aside for an hour.

3 When ready, cook the onions. Now put in the parsley, tomato sauce, egg and olives. Add pepper sauce and seasoning to taste. Stir to mix the ingredients well; leave to cool.

4 On a floured surface, roll out the dough to about ¼ inch/0.5 cm thick. Cut into circles with a saucer.

5 Spoon some of the mixture on one half of the dough circle. Top with grated cheese. Fold over the other half and seal by pressing with a fork.

6 Heat oil in a wok or deep-fryer and when hot cook the pasteis until golden on both sides. Remove and drain on absorbent paper. Serve hot.

Bolinhos de bacalhau (codfish balls)

SERVES 4-6   PREPARATION: OVERNIGHT SOAKING PLUS 20 MINUTES   COOKING: 40 MINUTES

A great snack, especially with a glass of cold beer. The cod needs to soak overnight in cold water.

½ pound / 225 g dried cod, soaked overnight
1 onion, sliced finely
2 tablespoons chives, chopped
2 tablespoons parsley, chopped
2 potatoes, cooked and mashed
2-3 tablespoons flour
1 teaspoon paprika
milk
oil
salt

1 Soak the cod overnight. Drain, and put the fish in a cooking pot. Cover with fresh water and simmer for 25 to 30 minutes. Remove the bones and skin, and then chop the fish finely.

2 Next, heat the oil in a frying pan. Add the onion and cook until it is soft. When the onion is translucent put in the chives, parsley and fish, stirring well. Continue to cook for a couple of minutes.

3 Now take the pan from the heat and add the milk, mashed potatoes, flour and paprika, adding a little milk if necessary. Combine well and check the flavoring; add a little salt if desired. Leave the mixture to cool.

4 When ready, take pieces of the mix and shape into walnut-sized balls or flat cakes. Heat up some oil in a frying pan or wok. Carefully slide in the fishballs and fry until golden. Drain on absorbent paper and serve hot.

Sopaipillas
(squash/pumpkin fritters) V

MAKES 12-15   PREPARATION: 10 MINUTES   COOKING: 5 MINUTES

Sopaipillas, sometimes called 'little pillows', are very similar to the Uruguayan *tortas fritas* but the big difference is that sopaipillas use pumpkin. This food, like *mote con huesillo* (peach drink), is typical of the central zone of Chile and is mainly eaten by poorer people.

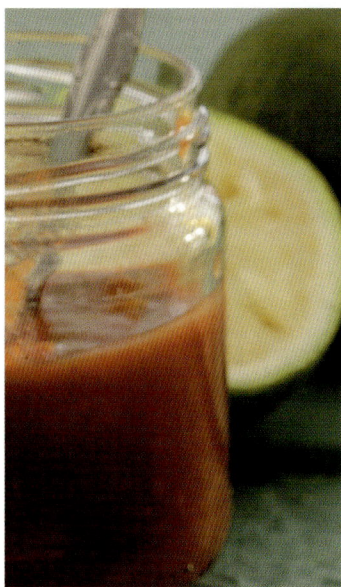

FOR THE *SOPAIPILLAS*:
2 cups / 200 g flour
1 cup / 100 g cooked
 pumpkin, drained
½ teaspoon cinnamon
salt
oil

FOR THE SYRUP*:
1 stick cinnamon or ½ teaspoon
 powdered cinnamon
peel of 1 orange, sliced thinly
1 cup / 240 ml water
½ cup / 100 g demerara sugar
1 clove

* In Chile, this would be *chancaca*, made of sugar cane.

1 Mash the cooked pumpkin and sift in the flour, cinnamon and a pinch of salt. Make a soft dough, kneading well.

2 On a floured surface, roll out the dough to about ½ inch/1 cm thick. Cut into fritter-sized pieces with a cookie cutter.

3 Heat the oil and when it is very hot, take up a fritter with tongs or a fork and fry briskly in the oil. Drain on absorbent paper and keep warm.

4 For the syrup, heat the water to boiling point and then add the sugar, cinnamon and the orange peel. Boil vigorously for 10 minutes or so, stirring all the time, until the sugar is dissolved and the mixture is beginning to caramelize. Remove from the heat.

5 Dip the sopaipillas in the hot syrup and serve immediately.

Bandeja paisa

SERVES 4   PREPARATION: OVERNIGHT SOAKING   COOKING: 40 MINUTES

La bandeja paisa is a local dish from Antioquia, Colombia's coffee region. This is a specialty of Medellín and you can purchase it at all the stalls. It's served hot on a clay plate. You can eat it with *arepa* – typical corn bread. In its original and most calorific form this dish serves *antioqueños* beans – beans cooked in the Antioquian way – and meat with white rice, pork fat, chorizo, fried egg, banana and beans. Sometimes it comes with a sauce, *el hogao*, made of onion with tomato sautéed on a very low heat until it becomes a soft paste. People enjoy freshly made fruit juices with the *bandeja paisa*.

1 cup / 175 g red kidney beans, cooked
½ pound / 225 g ground/ minced beef
1 cup *hogao* sauce* or tomato purée
¼ pound / 110 g bacon, sliced
oil
salt and pepper

*FOR 1 CUP/240 ML *HOGAO* SAUCE:
1 onion, chopped
6 tomatoes, chopped
water
salt and pepper

OPTIONAL SIDE DISHES:
4 eggs, fried
1 plantain, sliced and fried

1 To begin, make the sauce by heating a little oil in a pan and sautéing the onion for a few minutes until it is soft and golden. Then put in the chopped tomatoes and seasoning and cook very gently for 20 minutes or so until it is reduced and thickened. Add a little water and/or tomato sauce if it seems too stiff.

2 While that is happening, take another pan and lightly fry the meat in some oil for a few moments. Then add the hogao sauce and mix well. Set aside.

3 Fry or grill the bacon pieces until they are crisp. Drain on absorbent paper.

4 Now add the cooked beans to the meat and hogao mix and stir them in, partially mashing them as you do so. Heat through.

5 Serve on a plate with rice, the bean mix with the crispy bacon on top, and other ingredients as liked such as fried plantains, fried eggs and corn bread *arepas* (see p 138).

La Bomba

SERVES 4   PREPARATION: 5 MINUTES

Colombian people eat this – a sort of quick paella – at the weekend or before meetings or festivities because its ingredients give you energy. You can buy *La Bomba* in every streetmarket of Colombia's capital Bogotá and all around the country. It's very popular with young people, who might eat it before going out at night to dance, but adults consume it as well (and perhaps they also dance). The shellfish is often eaten raw, but you may prefer to cook it first.

Enough shellfish for 4 people (such as lobster, oysters, mussels, crab, shrimps)
4 tomatoes
1-2 tablespoons honey
juice of 1 lime or lemon
oil
salt

1 Put the tomatoes, honey and a pinch of salt into a blender and whizz to make a smooth sauce. Add a little lime or lemon juice and oil to make a smooth, thick sauce.

2 Put the shellfish into glass dishes. Spoon the sauce over it and serve cold, with crackers or bread.

Daiquiri (rum cocktail) V

MAKES 2   PREPARATION: 5 MINUTES

This is the basic daiquiri, but of course you can add fresh fruit juice or fresh fruit such as bananas or strawberries. *Daiquirí* is also the name of a beach near Santiago de Cuba, where workers from an iron mine used to drink a rum and fruit drink after work.

¼ cup / 60 ml rum
1-2 teaspoons sugar
juice of 2-3 limes
crushed ice

1 Place all the ingredients in a shaker or blender and mix. Adjust the tastes.

2 Pour over the crushed ice in a glass.

Mojito (rum cocktail) V

MAKES 2   PREPARATION: 5 MINUTES

Another Cuban classic.

¼ cup / 60 ml rum
juice of 2 limes
½ cup / 120 ml soda
  water
1-2 teaspoons sugar
sprig of mint
crushed ice

1 First, mix the lime juice with the sugar. Then add the mint and ice to this and combine well. Adjust the tastes and then divide between the glasses.

2 Now pour on the rum and top up with soda, stirring well.

Hornado de chancho (pork)

SERVES 8   PREPARATION: OVERNIGHT TO MARINATE *   COOKING: 2 HOURS *

This food is typical of Guaranda (a city about 300 kilometers south of Quito, the capital), but it is eaten all around the country as well. It is sold in every roadside stophouse. Street vendors often carry their wares onto buses and parade up and down the aisles to tempt passengers. They offer you a piece of newspaper to clean your mouth after you have eaten – that's a curious thing.

Chicha de jora is the maize brew made by indigenous people in the Andes – you can use beer instead. In Peru, *chicha* also means an informal arrangement, or a street vendor. In other Latin American countries, *chicha* can simply mean soft drink.

6 pound / 3 kg leg of pork
5 cloves garlic, chopped
1-2 cups / 470 ml *chicha de jora* or beer
1 teaspoon saffron or turmeric
2 teaspoons cumin seeds
1 teaspoon marjoram
2 tablespoons fresh basil
1 teaspoon salt
2 teaspoons pepper

* For a quicker version, use pork chops and marinate them for an hour or so before cooking, in their marinade, under a hot broiler or grill, for 20-25 minutes, turning once.

1 Prepare the marinade by blending the garlic with saffron or turmeric, cumin seeds, marjoram, basil, salt and pepper. Add enough chicha or beer to make a paste. Retain any remaining liquid for #3 below.

2 Rub the marinade mix all over the pork. Wrap the meat in plastic film or wax paper and leave in the fridge overnight.

3 When ready, pre-heat the oven to 325°F/170°C/Gas 3. Put the meat in a roasting dish and pour over any remaining beer or chicha. Cook the pork for approximately 2 hours until the skin is crisp and has a beautiful color.

Cheese pupusas

MAKES 10   PREPARATION: 20 MINUTES   COOKING: 10 MINUTES

Back in 1980, I remember *Pupusas de chicharon* (pork crackling), stuffed into one's mouth between charges of the riot police in the marches of 1 May, after Archbishop Romero's assassination in San Salvador. Or *pupusas de queso con loroco*, served under banana plants in the rain in northern Morazán, at the last bus stop before liberated territory. **Sean Hawkey, London, England**

½ pound / 225 g frozen pastry, thawed

½ pound / 225 g monterrey jack or
   cheddar cheese

1 onion, chopped

1 tomato

¼ cup / 50 g loroco +

¾ cup / 125 g beans, cooked

¼ teaspoon cumin

2 cloves garlic, chopped

¼-½ green chili, de-seeded and
   chopped finely

salt

+ optional

1 For the filling, fry the onion with the tomato, cumin, garlic and chili. Then add the cooked beans and mix well, crushing the beans. Next, chop the loroco, if using, and add it to the cheese.

2 Divide the dough into 10 pieces and roll each into a ball. Flatten each ball between the palms of your hands and press out to 3-inch/7-cm diameter discs.

3 Put a spoonful of the mixture in the middle of each disk of dough and top with the cheese-locoro mix. Enclose the *pupusa* by raising the sides of the dough around the filling and then seal it at the top. Flatten the *pupusas* again until they are about ½ inch or 1 cm thick.

4 To cook, heat a frying pan or skillet until it is very hot. Brush with a little oil. Cook the pupusas on each side for 4 to 5 minutes until nicely browned. Serve immediately, with *curtido* – cabbage salad (see below).

1 pound / 450 g cabbage,
   sliced finely

1 carrot, grated

6 scallions/spring onions,
   white part only, or 1
   onion sliced

1 teaspoon oregano

½ teaspoon chili powder

2 teaspoons brown sugar

½ cup / 120 ml vinegar

½ cup / 120 ml water

salt

Curtido (cabbage salad) V

SERVES 4-6   PREPARATION: 20 MINUTES PLUS 1 HOUR IN FRIDGE

This is the classic accompaniment to *pupusas* (above). The salad is piled on the plate with the *pupusas* on top.

1 Put the cabbage in a saucepan and cover with boiling water. Turn off the heat, and leave it to sit for 5 minutes, then drain well.

2 Now place the cabbage in a large bowl and add the grated carrots, scallions/spring onions, oregano, chili powder, brown sugar, vinegar, water and salt. Mix well and then put in the fridge for an hour or so. Serve with pupusas (above).

Jerk pork

SERVES 6   PREPARATION: 24 HOURS (12 HOURS FOR CHICKEN*)   COOKING: 1-2 HOURS

3 pounds / 1.5 kg
   tender pork, such as
   loin, or chicken *
1 Scotch bonnet or
   habanero pepper
1 onion
1 teaspoon allspice
1 teaspoon chili powder
1 teaspoon cayenne pepper
1 teaspoon black pepper
1 teaspoon sage
1 teaspoon thyme
1 teaspoon nutmeg
1 teaspoon cinnamon
4 cloves, heads only
3 cloves garlic, chopped
1 tablespoon sugar
1-2 tablespoons oil
1 tablespoon white vinegar
juice of 1-2 limes

The idea of jerk or jerked meat, with attendant 'rubs' or seasonings, conjures interesting images. The name 'jerk', similar to the US 'jerky', comes from an anglicization of the Spanish word *charqui*, derived from the Quechua Indian word *escharqui*.

While staying in the lush, green parish of Portland, I visited Port Antonio, considered the home of jerk. Both jerk pork and chicken were readily available, well seasoned with spices and cooked slowly over a pit of smoking pimento (allspice) wood. The 'Jerkman' served it in paper with 'festivals' – long, flat, slightly sweet, deep-fried dumplings – made from cornmeal (polenta).

There are many versions of seasonings or 'rubs'. The Scotch bonnet and *habanero* peppers are very hot, so use less if you wish. The meat is best cooked over a charcoal fire if possible – if not, use the oven. **Andy Hine, London, England**

1 To begin, put all the ingredients except the pork into a blender and blend to make a thick, smooth paste. Add more lime juice or water if required.

2 Place the meat on a non-metal baking dish and spoon the marinade all over, using your hands to rub it in. Wrap in aluminum foil and leave in the fridge for 24 hours – or 12 if using chicken.

3 If possible, slow-roast the meat over a barbecue. If not, use the oven (325°F/170°C/ Gas 3) and cook for 1-2 hours or until done.

Salsa casera (casera sauce) V

MAKES 2-4 SERVINGS   PREPARATION: 5 MINUTES

4 tomatoes, chopped
1 onion, chopped
2 cloves garlic
1 jalapeno pepper, de-seeded
   or use ½ teaspoon liquid
   jalapeno pepper
1 tablespoon cilantro/
   coriander, chopped
juice of 1 lime
salt

This is one of the many sauces and accompaniments for tacos (p 122). In addition to this uncooked salsa, there are cooked ones made with dried chilies, and a *tomatillo* salsa using small green tomatoes, as well as garnishes like onion, cilantro/coriander, guacamole and so on.

1 Put all the ingredients, except the lime juice, into a blender and mix. Add a little lime juice to obtain the taste and consistency you prefer.

2 Chill before using. The mixture will keep in a container in the fridge for up to a week.

Guacamole (avocado sauce) V

SERVES 4-6   PREPARATION: 5 MINUTES

This delicious cool green sauce is famous as an accompaniment to nachos. But it can be used on its own as a dip with sliced green or red bell peppers, carrots and so on.

2 ripe avocados
½ onion, very finely sliced
1 tomato, peeled and very
   finely chopped
2 cloves garlic, crushed
¼-½ teaspoon chili powder
juice of 1-2 limes or 1 lemon
1 tablespoon plain yogurt +
salt

+ optional

1 Slice open the avocados and remove the stone. Scoop the pulp into a bowl and mash well with a fork.

2 Combine with the onion, tomato, garlic and chili powder and mix well.

3 Now pour in the lime or lemon juice, and yogurt if using, and salt. Adjust seasonings and serve.

Tlacoyos azules (prickly pear dish)

MAKES 12-16   PREPARATION: 30 MINUTES   COOKING: 10 MINUTES

These are a seriously yummy, nutritious street food of Mexico City. They are only around at lunchtime: if you are there don't hesitate to eat one – and I assure you it will be more than just one. The *palmear* method of flattening the *tlacoyos*, see #3 below, takes time to master but don't let that stop you trying. You need to used refried beans – pinto beans cooked and put into a pan with a bit of oil or pork fat. When they're very hot you mash them. Let them dry; for this recipe you need them to be very dry. You can also make the filling with cottage cheese and some herbs – in Mexico that would be *epazote* but parsley will do. **Carlos Aceves Gaona, Canberra, Australia**

Harder to find is *nopales*, that is the 'leaves' or paddles of the *opuntia vulgaris* (prickly pear) cactus that gives the prickly pear fruit. You can buy this ready prepared (ie spines removed!) in jars on the internet.

FOR THE REFRIED BEANS:

1 cup / 200 g pinto beans, cooked

pinch of chili powder

oil

salt

FOR THE *TLACOYOS*:

1 pound / 450 g masa (corn/maize tortilla dough) *

1 cup / 200 g refried pinto beans (see above)

4 nopales, cut into two **

½ pound / 225 g fresh white cheese

spicy salsa

* *Masa azul* (blue masa) if possible.
** Available from gourmetsleuth. com – if you cannot obtain whole nopales leaves or 'paddles' use the chopped ones.

1 Start by making the refried beans. Heat a little oil in a pan and when hot put in the cooked beans. Stir them around to heat through and then mash with a fork. Add a little chili powder and salt. Make sure the mixture is dry before proceeding to #3.

2 Make the masa according to the packet instructions. Take a ball of dough (between a tennis ball and a ping-pong ball in size) in your hand and then put one finger in to make a hole.

3 Fill the hole with the refried beans paste. Once you fill the little ball you 'close' it. Then pass the ball from one hand to the other, pressing it a little each time to make it flat and an oval shape, about 4 inches/10 cm in length. The bean paste should only show a bit, so take care to press equally on each side to get the desired results.

4 As soon as you have made the tlacoyo, cook it on a hot griddle or flat pan with a smear of oil. When one side is done the bottom changes color and looks drier. Then flip to the other side.

5 Make cuts lengthwise on the nopales, but do not slice right through. If using sliced nopales, omit this step.

6 Place the nopal alongside the tlacoyo in the same pan, with no oil, and sprinkle with salt. Once cooked on one side, flip it over and add more salt. When it is cooked it softens, becomes a deeper green and has bits of black where it has caught while cooking.

7 Now put the nopal on top of the tlacoyo azul, and sprinkle with fresh cheese and some spicy salsa (see p 118).

Hot chocolate drink

FOR 2 CUPS   COOKING: 5 MINUTES

Rose-petal ice-cream, sold by the Zapoteca girls at the back of Oaxaca market is the taste of fun, a measure of just how far a society is prepared to go to enjoy food, and to enjoy life – a human happiness indicator that the UNDP should adopt. If ever I am facing a firing squad, this will be my final wish! It should ideally be washed down with dark hot chocolate served with a wooden whisk in a gourd, from the other side of the market where the chilies are. **Sean Hawkey, London, England.**

If you can find the ready-prepared *Ibarra* Mexican chocolate drink*, then look no further. However, if you do not have that, then follow this recipe, using non-sweetened cocoa as your base, not 'drinking chocolate' if possible.

* Available at gourmetsleuth.com

Cakes and desserts (*postres*) Oaxaca, Mexico.

4-8 teaspoons cocoa, depending on how strong you like it
2 teaspoons ground almonds
½ teaspoon cinnamon or 1 stick *
2 cups / 470 ml hot milk
sugar to taste

* If using stick cinnamon, put it in the saucepan as you heat the milk and remove it before serving.

1 Divide the ingredients between two cups or mugs. Pour on a little hot milk and stir to create a smooth and creamy paste.
2 Now pour in the remaining milk, stirring. Adjust the sweetness to taste.

Tacos filled with papas con chorizo (potato with chorizo)

FOR 12 TACO SHELLS OR TORTILLAS
PREPARATION: 10 MINUTES   COOKING: 20 MINUTES

Tacos are bought in markets or *tianguis* (a kind of street stall). This food is eaten by all social classes around Mexico, at any time. 'Taco' comes from a Spanish word meaning 'light snack'. But taco predates Europeans: Aztec and other peoples rolled tortillas or used them to scoop up food. The *campesinos* took their midday meal as tortillas wrapped around their food. Methods of preparation vary – *taquerias* (taco stands) and *puestos* (ambulatory carts usually in the same place each day) have different equipment. Whether the taco filling is fried, grilled or steamed depends on what is being used and each stand has its specialty. Tacos are a morning treat or night-time snack, not around much at gringo lunchtime.

Papas con chorizo is a popular filling but there are many others, such as *rajas*. This uses sliced *chile poblano* with cheese and cream. The *chile poblano* – 'chili of the people' – is a special kind of chili pepper: big and green, the most popular for use in tacos. It is usually cooked and peeled before use. Other popular fillings are cooked chicken or beans with flavorings such as chili.

12 taco shells or tortillas
2 cups / 300 g potatoes, cubed
1 chorizo, cubed or crumbled
1 tablespoon cilantro/coriander,
   chopped
1 tomato, sliced
salt

1 Cook the potatoes in boiling salted water. When they are tender, drain and place in a bowl. Mash slightly with a fork.

2 Heat a skillet or frying pan, then put in the chorizo and cook over low heat for 10 minutes, stirring from time to time.

3 Now add the potato to the chorizo in the skillet and stir round well so that the potato absorbs the chorizo fat.

4 Heat the taco shells or tortillas according to packet instructions. When ready, fill with the mixture. Garnish with cilantro/coriander and tomato before serving.

NICARAGUA

Gallo Pinto
(rice and bean tortillas) Va

SERVES 4-6   PREPARATION: 10 MINUTES   COOKING: 25 MINUTES

Gallo Pinto is a very typical Nicaraguan dish which is eaten daily, sometimes for every meal. This is a vegetarian dish which is so called because it resembles a speckled rooster – the *gallo pinto*. It is eaten at home but is also popular street fare and is delicious, nutritious and easy to cook. This quantity will make a meal on its own; serve half-measures for a tasty snack. **Helen Wallis, Swindon-Ocotal Link, England**

1 onion, chopped
3 cloves garlic, finely chopped
¾ cup / 110 g rice
½ pound / 225 g pinto beans, cooked
2 tablespoons cilantro/coriander, finely chopped
½-1 red chili, de-seeded and finely chopped or ½ teaspoon chili powder
1 cup / 240 ml soured cream or yogurt
8-12 flour tortillas
2 cups / 480 ml water
1 tomato, sliced
oil
salt

1 In a saucepan with a lid, start by frying the onion and garlic in the oil until soft.

2 Now add the rice and stir for a minute or so before adding the water. Cover, bring to the boil, and then lower the heat and simmer for 15-20 minutes, or until the rice is cooked.

3 When the rice is nearly ready, put in the cooked pinto beans and let them heat through with the rice.

4 Now scatter in the cilantro/coriander and chili and stir well. Cook for a couple of minutes. Garnish with the sliced tomato before serving with warm tortillas and soured cream.

This recipe comes from Swindon-Ocotal Link's (SOL) Nicaraguan recipe book. SOL is a charitable organization linking the communities of Swindon and Ocotal, Nicaragua. For more information or to order a recipe book please visit www.swindonocotal-link.org

Baho (meat and vegetable casserole)

SERVES 4   PREPARATION: 10 MINUTES   COOKING: 60 MINUTES

Baho is a very popular dish which is sold in street markets in northern Nicaragua. We were given this recipe by Ana Rosa Lopez, from Masaya. She cooks this dish in a huge metal container over a fire in Ocotal's busy market. In Nicaragua, banana leaves are used to line the base of the container to stop the food from burning. This dish is traditionally served with coleslaw (made with finely chopped white cabbage and carrots wrapped in mayonnaise). Cumin and cloves are commonly used as flavorings in Nicaraguan cooking. **Helen Wallis, Swindon-Ocotal Link, England**

1 pound / 450 g stewing/braising beef, chopped into small chunks or strips

3-4 potatoes, sliced

1 plantain or 1 banana, sliced

1 red bell pepper, cut into short strips

2 sticks of celery, sliced

3 tomatoes, sliced

1 large onion, sliced

4 cloves garlic, finely chopped

1 teaspoon cumin

4 cloves

½ orange, sliced +

3-4 teaspoons red wine vinegar

vegetable stock or water

oil

salt

+ optional

Heat oven to 350°F/180°C/Gas 4

1 Start by heating some oil in a pan and then sauté the meat pieces. Add the garlic. Fry until the meat is sealed and brown all over.

2 In a casserole dish, place the slices of plantain/banana on one side and the potatoes on the other. Add salt and place the slices of orange, if using, on top.

3 Now pour the meat and juices over the mixture, add the red wine vinegar and then pour in enough stock or water to just cover the meat. Sprinkle in the cumin and cloves at this point, if using.

4 Now put in layers of onion, bell pepper, celery and tomatoes on top. Add more salt to taste and cover with a casserole lid. Cook in the oven for an hour or until the meat is tender.

This recipe comes from Swindon-Ocotal Link's (SOL) Nicaraguan recipe book. SOL is a charitable organization linking the communities of Swindon and Ocotal, Nicaragua. For more information or to order a recipe book please visit www.swindonocotal-link.org

Chipa barrero (bread)

This typical food of Paraguay is sold in the streets everywhere, eaten by everyone. You can buy it on the bus when travelling from the capital Asunción to Caacupé, for example. *Chipas* sellers transport them in baskets. They are served at religious festivals. On the Day of the Dead, Paraguayans distribute *chipas* and sweets to children inside the cemetery, in the name of their ancestors.

It is reminiscent of the Brazilian *Pao de queijo*, the famous cheese bread from the state of Minas Gerais served at most steak houses in southern Brazil. The leavening is done by the steam during baking (in the way éclairs rise). These rolls should be eaten directly after cooking since they tend to collapse as they cool. In Brazil these rolls would be made with queijo de Minas, a mild, white cheese. **Jose Elosegui, Montevideo, Uruguay**

1 pound / 450 g cassava/manioc or maize/corn flour
¼ pound / 110 g margarine
4 eggs, beaten
½ pound / 225 g Paraguayan cheese, grated *
½ teaspoon anise
½ teaspoon salt
½ cup milk

*or use half parmesan and half white cheese such as Wensleydale.

Heat oven to 475°F/240°C/Gas 9

1 Start by mixing the margarine with the eggs; beat with a wooden spoon. Then add the grated cheese and anise.

2 Now dissolve the salt in the milk then add the flour. Spoon in the egg and cheese mixture and knead a little until it is just combined.

3 Shape small egg-sized pieces of the dough and place them on an oiled and floured baking sheet. Cook them in a very hot oven for 10 minutes, then reduce the heat and cook for a further 5-10 minutes.

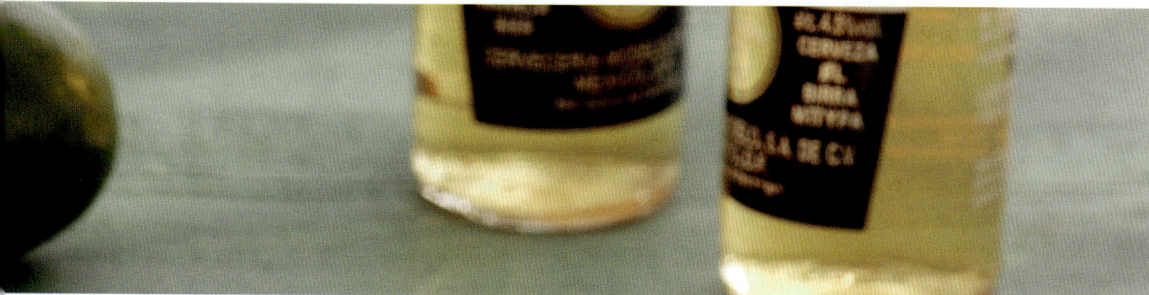

Cebiche de pescado (cebiche of fish)

SERVES 6-8   PREPARATION: 10 MINUTES PLUS 1 HOUR SET ASIDE

This is a famous Peruvian seafood dish. The Humboldt current keeps Peru's Pacific Ocean stocked with plankton, which attract many different fish. *Cebiche* has been on the menu for over 2,000 years. It's made with fish, scallops, shrimp or squid, or a mixture of these. Then marinated in lime juice with chilies and served raw with onion, sweetcorn and sweet potatoes.

The recipe is typical of the north of Peru but there are some special versions in the Ecuador border area. On both sides the 'black ostry cebiche' – another variety – is eaten with maize/corn. In Piura and Tumbes (Peru) and Huaquillas (Ecuador) there are lots of street markets selling *cebiche*. But each country has a different way of preparing it. Peruvians eat it with lemon and the Ecuadorians with milk and sauce.

1 pound / 450 g cod fillet, cut into small cubes
1 cup / 240 ml lime juice
1 clove garlic, crushed
½-1 teaspoon hot pepper sauce or 1 chili, de-seeded
1 onion, finely chopped
2 red bell peppers, cut into strips
2 sticks celery, finely chopped
2 tablespoons cilantro/coriander, finely chopped
1 sweetcorn cob per person
4 sweet potatoes
salt and pepper

1 Mix together the lime juice, garlic, pepper sauce and salt and pepper. Pour this over the fish and set aside to stand for 1 hour.

2 Now add the onion, red peppers, chopped celery and cilantro. Leave to stand for another hour.

3 When that is nearly ready, cook the corn and sweet potatoes and serve with the cebiche.

Pina colada (pineapple and coconut cocktail) ^V

SERVES 3   PREPARATION: 5 MINUTES

Made even more popular by a pop song, pina colada is one of the most common drinks in the region – you will find it everywhere in one form or another. And the reason for its popularity is easy to discover: if you're not sure, make one now and try it!

¾ cup / 90 ml rum
3 tablespoons coconut milk
3 tablespoons pineapple pieces
¾ cup / 90 ml pineapple juice
crushed ice

Blend everything, except the ice, together. Put the ice into glasses and pour the mixture over.

Chorizo al pan

FOR 1   PREPARATION: 5 MINUTES

Chorizo is a kind of meat eaten in many countries, but in Uruguay this food is part of popular culture and people are used to eating *chorizo al pan* in the street. The *chorizo* is a raw sausage made of different kinds of meats, which can be prepared with spices, salt and vinegar.

This food is sold in Uruguay particularly in the *carritos* – wheeled snack vans, like caravans, that are moved by car. There are lots of them on the streets of every Uruguayan city. Because of the wheels and the structure of the *carrito*, it is always higher than the people who frequent the stall, so the workers in the *carrito* must look down to see the customers.

Chorizo al pan is also sold widely at soccer matches from little stalls. In fact, it is sold every place where there are lots of people: friends' parties and get-togethers too. There have been changes with the years. Older people say that before, *chorizo al pan* was cooked only on the *medio tanque* (half an oil-drum on a stand as a barbecue or grill) and the bread was hard. Now we have the *carritos* and the *media luna* (a delicious kind of bread which is round). But a baguette would do. The *medio tanque* is still used in Uruguay. If somebody has a *parrilla* (grill) or a *medio tanque* at their house, their friends really appreciate it.

Chorizo al pan is so popular that it is eaten by all social classes and it is not expensive (less than one US dollar). It is sold in Argentina too but the Argentineans call it *choripan*. You can cook the chorizo in the oven, but Uruguayans prefer to cook them in the *parrilla* (grill) over the embers. You can also put the bread in the *parrilla* so it gets warm. After that, you cut the bread (a baguette would be good) in half to make two parts.
Jose Elosegui, Montevideo, Uruguay

1 chorizo, cooked
1 bread

1 When the chorizo is cooked, you slice it lengthwise but do not cut completely through, so that the sausage remains in one piece.

2 Then open it and place it between the bread. As the chorizo was not cut right through, it will not slide between the bread. Now press the bread a little so the chorizo cannot fall out. Add slices of tomato if desired.

Tortas fritas Va

MAKES 12-16   PREPARATION: 30 MINUTES

The *tortas fritas* are another typical Uruguyan food; part of the culture. They can be eaten at any time in the year but they are more special in winter because if somebody gets a *torta frita* which was cooked a few minutes earlier, it is warm and a potion against the cold day.

When there is a cold and rainy day Uruguayans will say, 'What a wonderful day to eat *tortas fritas*'. However, they are also eaten at every other season, including summer, when you can see people selling them in stalls by the beaches. Like the *garrapiñadas*, the *tortas fritas* are cooked and sold by vendors with their own gas stoves in little kiosks. The *tortas* are quite a heavy food so I wouldn't recommend eating too many in one day. They are usually eaten hot, with *mate* tea, coffee with milk, tea or milk with chocolate. Some people put sugar over the *torta frita* to make it sweet.

Happily, today *tortas fritas* are no longer sold as they once were. The kiosks had to be regulated because some were operating in unhygienic conditions. But now the street stalls are very clean. **Jose Elosegui, Montevideo, Uruguay**

2 cups / 200 g flour
2 teaspoons baking powder
½ teaspoon salt
1 tablespoon margarine
½ cup / 120 ml water
½ cup / 120 ml milk
oil

1 Sift together the flour, baking powder and salt into a large bowl. Then put in the margarine and mix it with the flour, using a fork to combine the ingredients.

2 Now add the liquids gradually, and then, with the hands, mix and knead everything until you have a very smooth dough that is not too stiff. When that is ready, set aside for 5 minutes, covered with a damp cloth.

3 After this, take small pieces of the dough and roll out each one to 3 inches/7 cm diameter. Prick the tortas with a fork.

4 Heat the oil in a wok or pan and fry the tortas on both sides. When they are nicely golden, remove and drain on absorbent paper.

Garrapiñada
(roasted peanuts) ^V

In Uruguay vendors have a gas stove and a little stall so they can cook *garrapiñada* in the street. When it is ready they put the *garrapiñada* in a small but long bag and give it to you. This allows the garrapiñada to slip down from the bag onto your other hand to be eaten – very handy.

All kinds of people eat this food, but the people who sell it in the street see this business as a way of getting money so they can eat every day. *Garrapiñada* is especially eaten in winter because you can get it seconds after it has been in the heat. The people who sell it are called *garrapiñeros* and some of them are moving to Argentina to sell their wares there too. **Jose Elosegui, Montevideo, Uruguay**

1 cup / 120 g roasted peanuts
1 cup / 175 g brown sugar
1 cup / 240 ml water
vanilla essence

1 If you have one, use a non-stick saucepan. Boil the water with the sugar for 10 minutes or so until the syrup begins to brown. Add a few drops of vanilla essence.

2 Next, put the peanuts in. Stir round with a wooden spoon and keep stirring until they are completely covered and the syrup begins to harden.

3 Remove from the pan and put spoonfuls on a plate to cool before eating.

Arepas V

MAKES 12   PREPARATION: 10 MINUTES   COOKING: 25 MINUTES

Arepas are served the moment they are ready. They can be filled with cheese, butter, meat, or scrambled eggs, for example. The *areperos* – sellers of the *arepas* – are in the city centers, where there are more people. Arepas are heavy on the stomach and too many people eat a lot of them at home at dinner time.

The Venezuelan singer Gualberto Ibarreto says in a song: 'My grandmother, not knowing geometry, cooked the arepas perfectly round'.

3 cups / 300 g white maize/corn flour
1½ cups / 360 ml water
½-1 tablespoon sugar
oil
salt

Heat oven to 350°F/180°C/Gas 4

1 Pour the water into a saucepan. As it heats up, add the salt, sugar and 1 tablespoon of the oil, and then gradually sift the flour in, trying to avoid making lumps.

2 Keep stirring and then kneading the mixture, adding more flour if necessary until you obtain a firm dough that does not stick to your fingers.

3 Make 2-inch/5-cm balls and flatten them slightly at the top and bottom.

4 Heat a lightly oiled griddle. When it is hot, put the arepas on it and cook until they have a golden brown crust on both sides. Keep separating them from the griddle or they will stick.

5 Then transfer them to a baking sheet in the oven and let them cook for 20 minutes or so, turning them from time to time, until they are golden and they make a hollow sound when you tap them. Serve with butter and grated cheese.

MIDDLE
NORT

Street café, Cairo, Egypt.

EAST &
AFRICA

EL AROS TEA

Fatayer bi sabanekh (spinach triangles) V

SERVES 4   PREPARATION: 15 MINUTES   COOKING: 15 MINUTES

Found everywhere on the streets of Beirut is *kaak*, a thick bread covered in sesame seeds and shaped like a purse. It is eaten with a handful of thyme or a slice of *picon* (processed cheese). Vendors push their carts through the streets, yelling 'kaak, kaak'– a cry that all Lebanese recognize immediately.

Another favorite is *fatayer* – these are dough shaped in a triangle and stuffed with spinach, lemon juice and salt. They can be baked or fried. **Reem Haddad, Beirut, Lebanon**

½ pound / 225 g frozen pastry, thawed
½ pound / 225 g spinach, finely sliced
1 onion, finely chopped
¼ teaspoon black pepper
1 tablespoon sumac powder
1 tablespoon pine nuts
juice of ½ lemon
oil
salt and pepper

Heat over to 450°F/230°C/Gas 8

1 Put the shredded spinach in a mixing bowl. Sprinkle a little salt over it and rub with your fingers until it wilts. Sprinkle the onions also with salt and then add pepper and sumac, pine nuts, lemon juice and olive oil. Mix well. Squeeze the spinach well in a colander to remove excess water, and then add it to the onion mixture. Set aside.

2 Roll out the dough on a floured surface to about ¼ inch/0.5 cm thickness. Cut into circles using a saucer.

3 Put a portion of the mixture onto the center of each piece. Bring up the sides to make a triangle. Dampen the edges a little and press them firmly together to seal.

4 Place on an oiled baking sheet and bake for 10-15 minutes, or until golden, and serve warm or at room temperature.

Hummus ^{Va}

SERVES 6-8   PREPARATION: 10 MINUTES

1 cup / 225 g chickpeas, cooked

4 teaspoons tahini

3 cloves garlic

juice of 1 lemon

1-2 tablespoons yogurt +

2 teaspoons sesame seeds +

¼ teaspoon paprika

½ tablespoon parsley, chopped

a few olives

olive oil

salt and pepper

+ optional

Hummus is popular around the region and widely available. The basics of chickpeas, tahini, garlic, lemon and olive oil can be modified and adapted to your taste – try it with added sesame seeds and yogurt. It is good served as an appetizer with pita bread or vegetables like carrots cut into sticks for dipping. Whether eaten in a Damascus market or in Alexandria on the Nile delta, this protein-rich dish is a classic – and its popularity has taken it all over the world.

1 In a blender, mix the chickpeas with the tahini, garlic, sesame seeds, lemon juice and yogurt, if using, adding a little olive oil as required to make a smooth paste. Season with salt and pepper and adjust the other flavorings as desired.

2 Scoop out the hummus into a bowl and scatter the parsley on top. Sprinkle on the paprika and decorate with a few olives. Serve with warm pita bread and carrot sticks.

GIACOMO PIROZZI/LPI

Boy with bread, Egypt.

Bathinjan mutabal
(egg-plant/aubergine dip) ^V

SERVES 4   PREPARATION: 5 MINUTES   COOKING: 20-30 MINUTES

Much of the street food in Beirut is sold on the seafront esplanade known as the Corniche. Built during the French mandate period, it is the crowded city's only breathing space. Here, hundreds of people come every day to walk up and down the seafront beside the sparkling water of the Mediterranean.
Reem Haddad, Beirut, Lebanon

1 egg-plant/aubergine
1-2 tablespoons tahini
1 tablespoon lemon juice
3 cloves garlic, crushed
**1 tablespoon parsley,
    finely chopped**
pinch of paprika +
salt and pepper

+ optional

1 Pierce the skin of the egg-plant/aubergine and bake or grill it, whole, for 20-30 minutes, turning from time to time.

2 When it is soft, let it cool a little and then remove the skin. Put it in the blender with the tahini, lemon juice and garlic and process to a smooth paste.

3 Spoon the mutabal into a bowl and garnish with parsley and a pinch of paprika.

Rangina
(dates in butter sauce) V

SERVES 6   PREPARATION: 10 MINUTES   COOKING: 5 MINUTES

A great dessert from the Gulf States – rich and delicious.

36 fresh dates, pitted
4 tablespoons butter
1-2 tablespoons flour
1 teaspoon crushed
** cardamom seeds**
2 teaspoons sugar +
6 whole almonds

+ optional

1 Divide the dates among 6 dessert bowls and place these in a very low oven.

2 Melt the butter in a pan, taking care that it does not catch. Stir in enough flour to make a smooth sauce and cook gently until the sauce turns golden brown.

3 Remove the sauce from the heat and stir in the cardamom. Pour over the warm dates and decorate with an almond before serving.

Hummus balila (chickpeas in olive oil) Va

SERVES 4   PREPARATION: 5 MINUTES

Some popular street foods in Lebanon are fava beans, piping hot roasted peanuts served in a magazine page rolled into a cone, some prickly pears, served peeled and on ice, *ful* and also *balila*, chickpeas with olive oil and lemon juice. You can use canned chickpeas – drained. **Reem Haddad, Beirut, Lebanon**

1 cup / 150 g chickpeas, cooked
  and kept warm
2 cloves garlic, crushed
2 tablespoons lemon juice
2 tablespoons margarine or
  butter, melted
½ teaspoon ground cumin
½ teaspoon ground cinnamon
2 tablespoons olive oil
¼ cup / 50 g toasted sesame seeds
salt

1 Put the warm chickpeas into a bowl.

2 Mix the garlic, lemon juice, cumin, cinnamon and melted margarine or butter. Add salt to taste. Pour this over the chickpeas and mix well.

3 When ready to serve, spoon over the olive oil and garnish with sesame seeds. Serve with tomatoes.

LEBANON

Batata bil kizbara
(potato with cilantro/coriander) ^V

SERVES 4   PREPARATION: 5 MINUTES   COOKING: 10 MINUTES

With a summer that lasts well into November, the Corniche promenade in Beirut is filled with people at all hours of the day and most of the night. Whole families set up camp, equipped with folding chairs, stove, coffee pots and *narghileh* (hubble-bubble pipe), and others just come to stroll or jog – and to eat. **Reem Haddad, Beirut, Lebanon**

1 pound / 450 g potatoes, cubed
4 cloves garlic
½ teaspoon paprika
½ teaspoon coriander
1 tablespoon toasted sesame seeds
4 tablespoons cilantro/coriander, chopped
lemon wedges
oil
salt

1 Parboil the potato pieces in a little water for 3 minutes. Drain well.

2 Heat the oil in a wok or frying pan and when it is hot, fry the potato pieces. Add the garlic, paprika, coriander, sesame seeds and 3 tablespoons of the cilantro/coriander.

3 Stir well to combine the ingredients, and then season with salt. Serve with the remaining cilantro/coriander on top, accompanied by the lemon wedges.

Almond cookies ^{Va}

MAKES 12-15   PREPARATION: 15 MINUTES   COOKING: 30 MINUTES

These are easy to make – a delicious tea-time snack. Almonds are one of Libya's main crops, along with olives, dates, citrus and cereals.

1½ cups / 150 g flour
1 cup / 100 g icing sugar
2 tablespoons butter or margarine
1 cup / 100 g ground almonds
¼ teaspoon almond essence
a little water

Heat oven to 350°F/180°C/Gas 4

1 Melt the butter or margarine in a pan and add the sugar with the almond essence. Stir well to mix and set aside.

2 In a bowl, sift in the flour and add the ground almonds. Now pour in the butter mixture and add a little water, stirring to form a crumbly consistency.

3 Grease a shallow baking tin. Spoon in the cookie mixture and spread evenly, pressing it down with a metal spoon to compact it.

4 Cut into squares or wedges, according to the shape of your baking tin, and then cook for 20-30 minutes until golden.

Falafel V

MAKES: 30 PATTIES   PREPARATION: 15 MINUTES PLUS 30 MINUTES SET ASIDE
COOKING: 5-10 MINUTES

A spicy patty made from dried beans, this is an excellent
vegetarian dish.

½ pound / 225 g fava beans, cooked
½ pound / 225 g chickpeas, cooked
3 cloves garlic, crushed
1 onion, finely chopped
2 scallions/spring onions, finely chopped
½ chili, de-seeded and finely chopped
1 tablespoon baking soda
3 tablespoons flour
1 teaspoon ground coriander
1 teaspoon ground cumin
2 tablespoons parsley, finely chopped
lemon wedges
oil
salt and pepper

1 Put the beans and chickpeas in the blender with the garlic, onion
and scallions/spring onions and blend to a thick mix.

2 Next, transfer the mixture into a bowl and add the baking soda,
flour, cilantro/coriander, cumin and parsley. Season and then cover
and set aside for 30 minutes or so.

3 Take a tablespoon of the mixture and form into patties about 1
inch/2.5 cm in diameter. Heat the oil in a wok and when it is hot, fry
the falafels until golden brown.

4 Serve with pita bread, tomato, and the lemon wedges.

Egg-plant/ aubergine salad ^V

SERVES 2   PREPARATION: 10 MINUTES   COOKING: 30 MINUTES

Cooked vegetable salads are found across the region. They keep well in the fridge and make both a good accompaniment to other dishes, or a snack on their own.

1 egg-plant/aubergine
2 slices bread, crumbed
3 cloves garlic, crushed
1 tablespoon lemon juice
1-2 tablespoons olive oil
½ onion, finely chopped
3 tablespoons parsley, chopped
salt and pepper
a few olives

1 Bake or grill the egg-plant/aubergine, after pricking the skin, until it is soft.

2 When it is ready, chop and combine it in a mixing bowl with the breadcrumbs. Add the lemon juice and olive oil and mash the mixture well.

3 Now put in the onion and parsley and seasoning. Mix well. Garnish with the olives and serve with hot pita bread.

Sfiha (meat pasties)

MAKES: 25-30 PIES   PREPARATION: 30 MINUTES   COOKING: 30 MINUTES

Meat pasties are found in many Middle Eastern countries such as Syria, Jordan, Lebanon and Iraq.

¾ pound / 350 g frozen pastry, thawed
1 pound / 450 g ground/minced lamb
1 onion, finely chopped
⅓ cup / 50 g pine nuts
½ teaspoon cinnamon
½ teaspoon allspice
3 tomatoes, chopped
3 tablespoons lemon juice
oil
salt and pepper

Heat oven to 350°F/180°C/Gas 4

1 Heat the oil in a large skillet/frying pan. When it is hot, put in the lamb and cook until the meat is crumbly and brown.

2 Now add the onion and sauté it before stirring in the pine nuts, spices and seasonings. Stir and cook for one minute.

3 Next, the chopped tomatoes go in. Cover the pan, reduce the heat and cook for 10 minutes until the tomato is soft. Remove from heat and pour in enough lemon juice to make a moist mixture. Set aside to cool.

4 Roll out the dough on a floured surface till it is ¼ inch/0.5 cm thick. Use a saucer to cut out circles about 3 inches/7 cm across. Place the rounds on a cloth and cover with another cloth.

5 Take a circle of dough and spread a spoonful of the mixture on one side. Close the patties and press the edges with a fork.

6 Put them on a lightly oiled baking sheet and bake for 15 minutes or until the crust is golden. Serve hot with fresh lemon or plain yogurt.

Grated carrot salad ^V

SERVES 2-4   PREPARATION: 10 MINUTES

Rose water gives this a delicate flavor, and its color adds cheer to any table. Rose petals are gathered to be distilled into rose water, used also in drinks and pastries.

½ pound / 225 g carrots, finely grated
pinch of salt
½ tablespoon sugar
½ tablespoon orange blossom or rose water
juice of ½ lemon
1 orange, peeled and sliced
olive oil

1 Place the grated carrots into a bowl.
2 Beat together the salt, lemon juice, sugar, orange blossom or rose water and oil. Pour over the grated carrot and decorate the bowl with the slices of orange.

MOROCCO

Harira (bean soup) ^V

SERVES 6   PREPARATION: 10 MINUTES   COOKING: 20 MINUTES

Morocco's national soup. During the period of Ramadan, every house prepares this perfumed soup, filling the streets with its scent at sundown. In Morocco, it is eaten along with dates, or honey sweetmeats (*chabakkia* with almonds and honey). There are many varieties of this soup; this is a meatless one.

1 cup / 175 g chickpeas or lentils, cooked

6 shallots, left whole, or use 2 onions, chopped

½ teaspoon saffron strands, soaked

½ teaspoon turmeric

½ teaspoon ginger

6 tomatoes, chopped

6 cups /1.5 liters water or stock

1 tablespoon tomato paste

2-3 tablespoons cilantro/coriander, chopped

2-3 tablespoons parsley

1-2 tablespoons flour

juice of ½ lemon

margarine or oil

salt and pepper

fresh dates +

+ optional

1 Start by putting the cooked chickpeas or lentils in a large saucepan. Add the shallots or onions, saffron, turmeric, ginger, tomatoes and tomato paste, as well as half the parsley and cilantro/coriander. Pour in the water or stock and add a blob of margarine or oil.

2 Bring to the boil, covered, and simmer gently to let the ingredients combine.

3 After 15 minutes or so, remove a little of the cooking liquid and mix it in a small bowl containing the flour, to make a smooth paste. Return this to the stewpot and stir well to mix it in. Pour in lemon juice to taste, and season.

4 Continue to simmer for 5 minutes, adjust seasonings, and serve with the remaining parsley and cilantro/coriander on top. Serve with fresh dates, if possible.

Avocado drink

MAKES 2 DRINKS   PREPARATION: 5 MINUTES

Morocco's *hleeb del laws* (almond milk) is a very
popular drink, and avocado milk is not far behind.

2 ripe avocados
½-1 tablespoon sugar
2 tablespoons condensed milk
8 ice cubes
a few mint leaves

Scoop the avocado flesh into a blender and add all the other
ingredients. Mix until smooth. Pour into glasses and decorate
with a few mint leaves.

Little shop, Tamanrasset, Algeria.

CLAUDIA WIENS/STILL PICTURES

Couscous V

SERVES 6   PREPARATION: 20 MINUTES   COOKING: 1 HOUR

3 pound / 1.5 kg chicken, cut into 6 pieces *

2 cups / 300 g couscous

½ cup / 80 g chickpeas, cooked

1 onion, chopped

1 egg-plant/aubergine, sliced

4 carrots, chopped

½ pound / 225 g pumpkin or squash,
    cut into 2-inch/5-cm pieces

4-6 tomatoes, chopped

1 green or red bell pepper, sliced

2-3 zucchini/courgettes, sliced

2 tablespoons parsley, chopped

2 tablespoons cilantro/coriander, chopped

1 teaspoon fresh or ground ginger

1 teaspoon turmeric

1 teaspoon cumin

2 cinnamon sticks

½ teaspoon chili powder or cayenne pepper

a few saffron threads +

3 cups / 750 ml stock

oil

salt and pepper

* You can omit the meat and replace with cooked
beans or vegetables if desired.
+ optional

This classic dish is found in many stalls in the souks of Marrakech and Fès. The mix of vegetables can be changed according to what you have available.

1 Combine chicken and stock in a large pan. Add the ginger, turmeric, cumin, cinnamon sticks, chili or cayenne,1 tablespoon of the parsley and cilantro/coriander, and a few drops of oil. Simmer until meat is cooked through (20-40 minutes), stirring from time to time.

2 Now put in the onion, tomatoes, carrot, pumpkin or squash, egg-plant/aubergine, bell pepper, zucchini/courgette and chick-peas. Sprinkle in salt and pepper to taste.

3 While that is cooking, put the couscous in a large pan and pour on enough boiling water to cover. Leave to stand until the water is absorbed, or follow packet instructions.

4 To serve, spoon the couscous onto a large serving plate. Make a well in the center and pile in the meat and vegetable mix, with some of the stock.

Tagine

SERVES 4   PREPARATION: 10 MINUTES   COOKING: 20 MINUTES

This Tunisian dish is like *eggeh*, a kind of omelet – very different from the Moroccan tagine, which is more of a stew. It is delicious, and can be eaten cold as well as hot.

1 onion, finely chopped
½ pound / 225 g chicken, cut into small pieces
1½ teaspoons tomato purée
1½ teaspoons paprika
1 cup / 240 ml water
1 cup / 150 g cannelloni beans, cooked
1 teaspoon butter or margarine
3 tablespoons parsley, chopped
1 cup / 100 g monterrey jack/cheddar cheese, grated
½ cup / 40 g breadcrumbs
4 eggs, beaten
¼ teaspoon cinnamon
2 tablespoons olive oil
salt and pepper

Heat oven to 350°F/180°C/Gas 4

1 Begin by heating the oil and then sauté the onion. Put olive oil and onion in a saucepan and place over medium heat. When the onions are translucent, add the pieces of chicken meat and brown them on all sides.

2 Now put in the tomato purée, paprika and water and cook gently for a couple of minutes. Then add boiling water and simmer for 5 minutes or so, to create a thick sauce.

3 When ready, add the beans and simmer for a few minutes to heat them through. Then add a layer of cheese, parsley, breadcrumbs and cinnamon. Season; mix well, and adjust the seasonings and flavorings to taste.

4 Grease a baking dish with the margarine or butter. Spoon in the mixture and pour the beaten eggs on top. Bake for 15 to 20 minutes or until the top of the tagine is lightly crisp and the eggs are set. Serve warm, cut into wedges, with a salad.

Mechouia
(grilled vegetable salad) ^{Va}

SERVES 6   PREPARATION: 10 MINUTES   COOKING: 20 MINUTES

This tasty and colorful cooked vegetable salad from Tunisia is easy to make. It can be used to fill sandwiches, baguettes or pita bread.

2 red bell peppers
1 red onion, sliced in circles
4 tomatoes, halved
juice of ½ lemon
olive oil
1 teaspoon oregano
2 hard-boiled eggs, sliced +
a few olives
olive oil
salt and pepper

+ optional

Heat broiler/grill, or oven to 400°F/200°C/Gas 6 – see #1 below.

1 Grill the whole bell peppers, tomatoes and onions in a hot oven for about 20 minutes, or under the broiler/grill. Turn them over from time to time to char on all sides and cook until they are soft. Remove from the grill or oven and allow to cool.

2 When ready, remove the seeds and stalks from the peppers. Chop them, the tomatoes and onions into small pieces. Arrange them on a flat plate.

3 Mix together the lemon juice, olive oil, oregano, salt and pepper and pour this over the grilled vegetables. Serve garnished with the hard-boiled eggs and olives on top.

Resources and contacts

Penang Food Odyssey by Yvonne Tan (Penang 2000; ISBN 983-40269-0-0). This delightful book is full of useful information about the food and the people who sell it in Penang.

World Food series (Lonely Planet Publications Pty Ltd, Hawthorn, Victoria, Australia; various authors/publication dates, www.lonelyplanet.com). These are great little books, easy to pack on your travels, with lots of tips and cultural background.

Thai Hawker Food by Kenny Yee, Catherine Gordon and Sun Win (Clive Wing/ Book Promotion & Service, Bangkok, 2001, www.book.co.th)

Hawkers Delight: a guide to Malaysia and Singapore's Hawkers' Food (S Abdul Majeed & Co, Kuala Lumpur, Malaysia, 2004).

Homestyle Filipino Cooking by Norma Chikiamco and other titles (Periplus Editions [HK] Ltd, 2003 and other dates).

The Congo Cookbook – great collection of African food ideas, plus fascinating information and historical/cultural background to foods, www.congocookbook.com

www.gourmetsleuth.com – all the ingredients you cannot find elsewhere.

Consumers' Association of Penang – campaigning organization. 228 Jalan Macalister, 10400 Pulau Pinang, Malaysia. email: meenaco@pd.jaring.my

Health Action International – working to improve access to essential medicines. www.haiweb.org

Oxfam International – campaigns on Fair Trade and promotes organic farming. www.oxfam.org

Food and Agriculture Organization – information on all aspects of food. www.fao.org

The Vegetarian Society www.vegsoc.org

The Vegan Society www.vegansociety.com

Food stalls, Penang, Malaysia.

Natural Resources Institute at the University of Greenwich, Medway, England. Studies on street food vending. www.nri.org

Fair Trade

The International Federation for Alternative Trade (IFAT) www.ifat.org
IFAT members who sell some of the ingredients for recipes in this book:
Australia: Community Aid Abroad Trading www.caatrading.org.au
Britain: Traidcraft Exchange www.traidcraft.co.uk
Canada: Level Ground Trading Ltd www.levelground.com
Japan: Global Village Fair Trade Company www.globalvillage.org.jp
New Zealand/Aotearoa: Traid Aid Importers Ltd www.tradeaid.org.nz
US: Equal Exchange www.equalexchange.com

Fair Trade Labelling Organization (FLO) monitors traders using the fair trade mark.
www.fairtrade.net
Britain: The Fairtrade Foundation www.fairtrade.org.uk
Canada: Transfair www.web.net/fairtrade
Europe: Max Havelaar www.maxhavelaar.nl
Ireland: Fairtrade Mark Ireland www.fair-mark.org
Japan: TransFair www.transfair-jp.com
US: TransFair www.transfairusa.org

Organic farming campaign groups
Soil Association www.soilassociation.org
Friends of the Earth www.foei.org
Greenpeace www.greenpeace.org

If using eggs and meat, purchase free range and organic only.
See Compassion in World Farming (CIWF) for further information.
www.ciwf.org.uk/

TROTH WELLS/NEW INTERNATIONALIST

Menu at Sushila's, Penang, Malaysia.

173

Index of recipes and main ingredients

About the author

Troth Wells joined the NI in 1972, helping to launch the *New Internationalist* magazine and build up its subscriber base. She now works on the editorial team as Publications Editor and has produced five food books including *The World in Your Kitchen* (1993), *The Spices of Life* (1996) and *The World of Street Food* (2005). In addition she is the English-language editor of *The World Guide*, produced by the Third World Institute in Uruguay. She has travelled in Central America, Africa, India and Southeast Asia.

About the New Internationalist

The New Internationalist (NI) is a not-for-profit co-operative based in Oxford, UK, with associated offices in Adelaide, Australia; Toronto, Canada; Christchurch, New Zealand/Aotearoa; and Dublin, Ireland. Founded in 1972 with the backing of Oxfam and Christian Aid, the NI has been fully independent for many years. It publishes the *New Internationalist* magazine, with 75,000 subscribers worldwide, which reports on global issues, focussing on the unjust relationship between rich and poor worlds. The NI also produces publications including the *One World Calendar*, the *No-Nonsense Guide* series to topical political issues; food books such as *The World in Your Kitchen*, and photo books including *Water, life force*.
www.newint.org